Mysterium Australis

III

The Return of the Templars

Christian Karma,
Public Service
and Future of the West

Héraclès Harixcalde

Volume 3

Mysterium Australis

Return of the Templars

Christian Karma, Public Service and Future of the West

1st edition

En application de l'art. L.137-2.-I. du code de la propriété intellectuelle, toute reproduction et/ou divulgation de parties de l'œuvre dépassant le volume prévu par la loi est expressément interdite.

© Héraclès Harixcalde, 2025

Publisher : BoD · Books on Demand, 31 avenue Saint-Rémy, 57600 Forbach, bod@bod.fr
Print : Libri Plureos GmbH, Friedensallee 273, 22763 Hamburg (Allemagne)

ISBN : 978-2-3225-7802-3
Legal deposit : Juin 2025

« I am the problem and the solution; I hold the totem and the Eye of Horus. »

VALD

« Memento mori. » (Remember you will die)

Inscription au sol, South Leith Church Parish, Ecosse

« A civilization that wages war, divides into classes, and hates races is not the product of one man, but of all men. No man can say: 'I am good, therefore I did not create it. »

Lao Russell, Dieu travaillera avec vous mais pas pour vous.

« Normality is a paved road: it is easy to walk, but no flowers grow there.»

Vincent van Gogh

« When the blackbird sees the grape harvesters enter the vineyard, he is most surprised to see that they, unlike him, are not afraid of the scarecrow. »

Jules Renard

Preamble

In this final volume of *Mysterium Australis*, drawing on my personal experience and the teachings of the previous volumes, I will attempt to expose all the invisible threads that govern the West and prevent its entry into the new Golden Age, with a Focus on France and UK. Indeed, while on an individual scale it seems to each of us that we are on the right path and at the peak of civilization—thanks to technological progress and AI in a so-called "Judeo-Christian" West—we are right to question this when we look at the fruits we have borne over the past 50 years in terms of architecture, craftsmanship, clothing, and customs. These are primarily the consequences of the veneration of a new golden calf that drives everyone to chase the fruit rather than grow the branch...

Here, we will first find the conclusion of *Logan's Apocalypse*, with the final part of Volume 2, which wraps up the revelations about my ancestry (Logan of Restalrig) and recounts my road trip across the "United Kingdom" in a chrome blue Volkswagen camper van—from London to Edinburgh—my discovery of the secret of the Templars, and my exchanges with Abraxas, Helios, or with that being who communicates through symbols and synchronicities... The reader will come to understand the role of the English crown, in complicity with speculative Freemasonry and the Reformed Church, in the establishment of the global control web we have already addressed many times. Beware, here we are at the edge of the world, dealing with the very construction of reality. I will simply recount the facts here in the same style as Volume 2, and we will deepen the concepts and offer paths to understanding in the second part, as all this may seem abstract and frightening to a reader not versed in theology, mysticism, and esotericism.

I will try to show you that, due to a somewhat twisted original design of Christianity, multiple modifications to its dogma, a messy and poorly translated biblical corpus, and various schisms and ecumenical councils, we find ourselves at the very end of the Dark Age (or Kali Yuga). This is an age ruled by the Devil because we have abandoned the study of God's language—Ancient Greek. The Golden

Age struggles to begin because of the grim stories told about the Apocalypse. For it is ultimately the stories we tell ourselves that govern the world, and one can easily understand the perverse imbalances that a society may suffer from when it has abandoned both parents and children to the television—which still largely controls our reality today. How to overcome this? Should we organize a bonfire of our TV screens? You'll see that even the Devil has had enough of his own devilry, and that he himself is conspiring to resurrect the old gods—or the Archons. Each of us must recognize and take responsibility for our share, our own faults, while also accepting the shadow that characterizes us all—the serpent, the *noûs* that grows in the dark with each of our actions, which we can no longer ignore. And thus, perhaps, Zeus will pass the torch to Dionysus.

Since everything is connected—that's the essence of religion—and religious organizations are above all just that: organizations, meaning hierarchically structured groups of men, I will extend the scope of this study to society at large, and to France in particular, as it is the example I know best. This model can be more or less transposed to the United Kingdom, Australia, and Canada, which are the last bastions of the Dark Age, whose problems primarily stem from abusive bureaucracy and a lack of leadership. I will take the opportunity to propose the only solution I believe to be viable for saving these states and our civilization in the long term—a plan that will take about twenty years to implement but could certainly breathe new energy into these societies that already feel like they're drowning.

With the aim of reaching a broad audience, and because modernity allows us to verify sources ourselves, I will keep my usual style and avoid falling into academic study. I will simply cite the sources and authors in the text, positioning myself in a subjective register that, I believe, will resonate with the greatest number and also, because as usual, I am writing this under pressure of the perpetual war we have entered and asks for an ending.

Table des Matières

Book I – Logan's Apocalypse (end)

    Part 4 – Awakening Road-trip to Alba.............. p.11

Book II – The Return of the Templars

Part 1 – Spiritual issues ans solutions p.63
    God, Irrationality, and the Druid
    Genesis and Hermetic Philosophy
    Giordano Bruno, the Stake, and the Apocalypse
    How Does Mysticism Work?
    Introverts, Schizophrenics, Bipolars: Poor Mages
    Pigeons and Seagulls
    The Spanish Family: A Model to Repair the Mystique
    How We Care for the Elderly?
    How We Celebrate Our Dead
    Islam
    Judaism and antisemitism
    Speculative Freemasonry
    Women Will Be Women When Men Are Men
    Templars Treasure: Healthy Frequencies and Sacred Geometry
    Jesus Christ: The First Attempt to Establish Western Buddhism?
    Celtic Church, "Buddhist Tradition," Decentralized Christianity
    The Holy Grail: What If It Was Logan of Restalrig?
    The English Crown (Once Again) Killed Christ
    A Low-Quality Electromagnetic Broth
    Stonecutters Forge our Souls
    Christianity: Paradox of the Vatican and New Golden Age
    Marie, Isis and Sophia
    Freeing Christian Karma or Disappearing as a Civilization
    Drawing a Line on the Past and Forgiving
    Veritas, Sacrificas, Immortalitas, Libertas

Sons of Abraham, but not only: on the need of a Greek oral tradition akin to the Jewish one
Henry IV and His Château (intermission)
A unique Solution: The Red Book
Pleroma, New Aeon, and Philosopher's Stone
Conclusion: Templars for Feathered Snake

Part 2 – Organizational issues and solutions..........p.118
Saint Germain-en-Laye, Le Laurain and Napoléon
The Left/Right Divide
COVID-19: Real Consequences of an Imaginary Pandemic
A Perfect Example: The City of Pau
A Quick Guide to the Stasi
The British Example
The Subverted West and the Discreet Yellow Peril
Social Services and Child Protective Services (ASE)
Mafia-like unions and the bad example of the SNCF
The Environmental Diktat
The Parasitic Bureaucracy
The Prefecture
The Civil Code and the Law
The High Judiciary Council
Punishment and Death Penalty
The Funding of NGOs
Military Service and a new Elite of Consciousness
Old Cities vs. Modern Cities
Operative Freemasonry
Borders, Integration, and "Social Nationalism"
Return of Craftsmanship and Local Cultures
The Potlatch and the Village Fair
Solving the Monetary Problem
Solving the Accounting Monarchy
A Unique solution: Operative Monarchy
Conclusion: Too Many Public Services Kills Public Services
General Conclusion

Book 1

Logan's Apocalypse

How to catch a Leviathan?

(end)

Part IV

Awakening road-trip to Alba

Ambivalent Verb, May God Gather

*The Logos was split like a seed;
In silence, the One was torn apart.
A Voice was born from Pain,
And a Music from the Fall—
A red thread through Chaos.*

*Each letter is a scrap of fire,
Each sound, a remembrance.
Through the rift,
The mystic pierces toward the unspeakable;
The broken becomes a key, and
The Antilogos a supreme good.*

*The Logos, like lightning, divides and enlightens.
Do not flee contradiction;
within it, God is hidden.*

Λόγος δυόφων θεῶν ἀγορήν

Ὁ Λόγος ἐσχίσθη ὥσπερ σπέρμα·
ἐν σιγῇ ἐσπαράγη τὸ Ἕν.
Καὶ φωνή ἐγεννήθη ἐκ πόνου·
μουσικὴ ἐκ πτώσεως,
μῖτος ἐκ χάους.

Ἕκαστον γράμμα πυρὸς ῥάκος,
ἕκαστος φθόγγος ἀνάμνησις.
Διὰ τῆς διακοπῆς,
ὁ μύστης εἰσέρχεται πρὸς τὸ ἄρρητον·
Τὸ σχισθὲν γίνεται κλεὶς·
ὁ ἀντίλογος ἀγαθόν.

Ὁ λόγος ἐστιν ὡς ἀστραπή· διαιρεῖ καὶ φωτίζει.
Μὴ φεῦγε τὴν ἀντίφασιν·
ἐν αὐτῇ κρύπτεται ὁ Θεός.

Logos Dyophon Theon Agoras

Ho Logos eschisté hospér spérma;
en sigeé esparagé to Hen.
Kai phoné egennéthé ek ponou;
mousike ek ptoseos,
mitos ek chaous.

Ekaston gramma puros rhakos,
ekastos phthoggos anamnesis.
Dia tes diakopes,
ho mustēs eisérchetai pros to arréton;
To schisthen ginetai kleis;
ho antilogos agathon.

Ho logos estin hos astrape; diairei kai photiozei.
Me pheuge ten antiphasin;
en autée kryptetai ho Theos.

29

"I do not understand travelers who use the world like a couch, and who insult the road by turning it into the therapist of their neuroses."

Sylvain Tesson

A shovel and a crowbar in the satchel slung across my shoulder, I was parked on the outskirts of Lochend Park in Edinburgh, patiently waiting in the back of the chrome-blue rental Volkswagen Transporter for the regular pendulum—where the descending sun gives way to the moon—to complete its course. I'd had little sleep these past days, yet my *soma* was in perfect shape. It seemed I had indeed been repaired, for I couldn't recall ever having felt so well—fully recharged with a *mana* whose secrets I'd never previously known...

I was pondering this and that, wondering how best to calmly put into words the past few weeks of travel, which had felt outside of time and more guided by providence than by any strict itinerary—like those I used to prepare in my younger years, carefully planned out as a couple for a limited-time trip. Now, life appeared to me as a journey without an end. I listened intently to the fridge, or the battery, or some unknown piece of electrical equipment in the van that activated at regular intervals, helping guide my thoughts—and I'd come to the conclusion that this faulty rental van was, in a way, a divine intermediary: the *daimonion* or the *daimon*, the one described by Sophocles and Plato in their stories, who aids them, in their divine madness, in making important decisions...

I had bought the crowbar and the shovel at a hardware store called Screw Fix near the park, and I had just stocked up on lentils, ginger, and beets, because, as the fateful hour of the treasure's discovery approached, I had been warned via push notification that the whole north-west of Spain—which, incidentally, is highly dependent on renewable energy and has remained outside the European energy market—had just experienced a massive power outage, most likely due to a cyberattack. Sensing the fall and the likelihood of power cuts spreading across Europe, as I had told the Screw Fix vendor, I was anticipating a period of chaos followed by a return to the Middle Ages, which, to be honest, rather delighted me. I had in mind scenes of mutual aid, the village fair, jugglers, community gatherings, nighttime vigils lit by candles and torches, unique encounters, and a daily life no longer marked by routine, where sleepwalking people are shuttled around on conveyor belts through overcrowded train stations.

As a precaution, I also bought protective goggles and a gas mask—precautions I had picked up during the East Coast wildfires in Australia with MT, masks that had suddenly become very valuable at the time... In Pau, I had already noticed some very strange power outages, flashes without electricity, and longer blackouts that had never really been explained and looked a lot like what might happen if you left a child—or Macron—alone in front of a big red button and told him: "whatever you do, don't press this button." This particular blackout was more serious, it was severely affecting transportation, and I was already receiving messages on my phone saying that French public transport would also be impacted by the time I got back. Nothing too unusual, all things considered, with railway workers and public transport strikes.

Despite this unusual event, I was convinced that God had shown me the location of the Templar treasure, and nothing could divert me from my objective. Although I had already suspected that this treasure was not what people believed it to be—made of gold and rubies—I still secretly nourished the hope of a divine reward for the trials I had endured. Oh, pride, when you hold us tight... Some kind of instant gift, as I had received a few times throughout my journey.

Lochend Park was located in the Restalrig district of Edinburgh, a neighborhood lying at the foot of Holyrood Park, which serves as the backdrop of the city, visible from almost anywhere with its rocky, yellow-green vegetation. At the entrance of the park stood a plaque—the only place over the past two weeks where I had seen the name Logan of Restalrig mentioned. At the center of the park was a loch and its old water pump, which once served as the city's main water source, before Edinburgh expanded so greatly that the pump was declared insufficient. According to rumors, this loch was bottomless. People had tried throwing weighted objects into it to determine its depth, but they were never recovered. In the middle of the loch, the branches of aquatic trees were slowly reclaiming their ground, and ducks and geese carved their paths through it—always quick to indicate to me, with their cries, whether I was heading in the right or wrong direction. Overlooking the park stood Lochend Castle, once called Restalrig Castle, though nothing remained of the original stronghold but a single building—the façade facing the park, perched some ten meters above a rocky wall that could easily be climbed.

That afternoon, during my scouting and data collection, I had climbed the wall, only to realize afterward that access to the park was open, so I decided to approach the front door to see whether a visit was possible. I walked up calmly, raising an open hand to the man who was standing there. It seemed the place was occupied by residents of various origins, and I was received by a man who first introduced himself as Spanish, then told me he was from Mauritius. When I asked whether I could visit, he threatened me while pointing at the cameras. I asked what this place was and who managed it, and I learned it had become a shelter for children and foreigners, run by the Cameron Guest House Group. I understood they didn't want shady strangers approaching the children, but I cast one last glance at the cameras, which seemed to me to be those cheap fake ones—the kind installed like scarecrows rather than the ones you find everywhere else in the UK, linked to a control center—and I couldn't help but think of Saruman... A quick search about this organization confirmed my suspicions: it was just another money-sucking government machine, and its greedy managers were wallowing in useless riches.

I politely took leave of the employee and left without causing too much trouble, heading back to the cliff behind the building. And there, to my great surprise, I found a completely ordinary man— Scottish—lying at a 75-degree angle in a very uncomfortable position among the bushes on a bed of leaves. I called out to him, surprised, asking what he was doing there. He first replied that he was trying to sleep, but it was 2 p.m., and not satisfied with that answer, I pressed on, laughing a little: "But what are you doing here?" He eventually confessed that he had fled from his wife and was taking a break, which, of course, earned him my sympathy. I introduced myself: "I am Logan of Restalrig. This is my castle. They've turned it into a migrant shelter. Don't you feel like storming it with me?" And he replied with something like, "Ahh, the bastards." I noticed a rear window whose coating looked freshly applied, and I decided to gently remove one pane to open the window from the outside and have a look at what was going on inside. But the Spaniard, on high alert, immediately rushed to the window as soon as I touched the glass and threatened to call the police. I replied that I was just picking up a few stones from the cliff, that I was a collector, and that this old building was my ancestors' home. He retorted that the building was a hundred years old, and I hastened to correct him, saying it was much older than that. The scene—between the Spaniard from Mauritius and the sleeping Scotsman—was becoming completely absurd, so I decided to forget about the castle, at least for now.

I went back down around the edges of the lake and resumed following the signs… which led me to the foot of another cliff, beneath a large plane tree where, on a mound of earth, lay three asbestos sheets that suggested to me that the treasure was buried there. Armed with this essential information, I returned to the van to wait for evening.

After a nap and some wandering thoughts, I went back to the mound, set up my lamp, and made sure no one had followed me. In the afternoon, many passersby asked me unusual questions. This place was now surrounded by social housing and other developments, and while some had their routine health walks in the park to enjoy nature, it seemed others besides me had narrowed the search area and were noting every unusual passage, or trying to extract information about a potential treasure from any strange faces they could encounter there.

When you embark on a treasure hunt, there are two essential prerequisites: to be very sure of your instincts, and to love digging. So I began to dig into the mound, digging in the dark for one meter, and found nothing. Had I been fooled? Had my daemon mocked me again? In the dark, it was hard to make out anything... the stones seemed like simple stones, but was that certain? To be sure, I filled the square UberEats bag I had found earlier, very practical both as a cover—making me look like a delivery person—and for carrying the loot. After an hour digging with my small camping shovel, I took a break and began to doubt the wisdom of my endeavor, wondering if maybe it was my French side to believe in treasures, as the French soldiers of La Pérouse's first expedition to Australia had done, whose map was drawn by someone close to the English crown and showed buried treasures on nearby islands—an irresistible lure of greed that caused the French to arrive too late to claim the Australian territory... leaving the field open for the British convict expedition. The course of the world might depend on small mistakes, though I doubted it and thought it was more of a subtle design. I resumed digging, a second meter, and picked up a few more rock samples. At last, I began to feel the edges of an object and immediately thought of a chest, like those I remembered from my *Return to Monkey Island* game sessions, and, looking back, my adventures seemed to take on a similar tone...

I dug all around the shape, long and rectangular, about 1 meter long and 30 centimetres wide, weighing around 70 kilos, and I increasingly sensed it wasn't a chest but a stone. On the stone, I noticed some markings like those I had seen on church stones—signs that resembled Viking or Egyptian symbols, used to identify the stonecutter for signature and payment.

I placed a tree stump beside the large stone and, using the crowbar, I applied leverage to lift the treasure out of the earth, in this two-by-two-meter hole. The treasure, a large rock, was the same stone used in the coronation of the kings of Scotland—known as the Stone of Destiny—a red sandstone. I had seen it in Perth, the one they exhibited. They said it was Jacob's stone, or the pillow of Jacob from the Bible. The stone had a long history, and recently Charles III had brought it from Scotland to Westminster for his coronation, because he had to sit on it—it proved he was king of Scotland. For a long time, the stone was kept at Westminster, until in the 1950s, Scottish independence students organized to steal it and bring it back to Scotland, hiding it and then depositing it in a ruined castle—the Abbey of Arbroath—before it was finally displayed at the Perth Museum. At the beginning of the century, on two occasions, socialist women had tried to blow it up, and it ended up broken in two. That shows the power of a symbol attached to a mere rock. This was THE rock. After all, how to prove that the stone displayed in Perth was really Jacob's pillow? In my view, if it was anywhere, it was hidden underground until the return of Restalrig. Logan of Restalrig had always possessed the other stone—it was the fake one. The seventh Logan of Restalrig, at the end of the 16th century, knowing he was in trouble with the English crown, had taken precautions and distributed as much of his fortune as possible to his close ones, and had hidden the Stone of Destiny here, for his future descendant to find.

After exerting all my strength to extract this stone from the hole, exhausted, I sat down on the stone for five minutes before realizing it was nearly midnight and my train left London at 2 p.m. Relatively satisfied with my find, I took the way back. Empty pockets and a full heart.

30

- Solomon: *"Life is so much easier to live when you're dead."*
- Tommy Shelby: *"I'll keep going until I find a man I can't defeat."*

Peaky Blinders

After publishing Volume 2 of *Mysterium Australis*, I decided to spend a few days in Paris before the road trip to England, staying in an apartment that a friend on vacation had lent me in the 18th arrondissement. I didn't yet know that the next stage of my initiation had already begun.

I took the opportunity to visit bookstores where I left my books on consignment and to consult some rare books in the national libraries. I started with the Arsenal Library, at the corner of Rue de Sully and Rue Henry IV. The atmosphere was studious and formal, without frills but solemn. After being greeted with suspicion because of my kilt, they kindly made me a library card once I mentioned the name "Gabriel Naudé," the former librarian of Mazarin, whose descendant I had recently met. I thought to myself that these librarians were the true deep state.

Unfortunately, the book I was looking for was not there, but I saw it on the shelves at Richelieu and went there immediately by metro. A very grand and well-stocked library stood there beneath the gaze of a statue of Molière, extremely frequented for its architecture and studious by its impressive number of books and study rooms. I wanted to consult the theology book which strangely appeared in the "Coins" section. Unfortunately, the book was in the reserves, and the strikes made access to the stock impossible, but I was told that the book was available on the shelves at the François Mitterrand Library. Coming out of the François Mitterrand station, the esplanade of the modern district was empty that Saturday. The library, a building designed like two concrete books opened and placed in a hollow of vegetation, matched the forests and green spaces that now grew across the large square near City Hall and elsewhere. From the interior glass windows, one could see, here and there through the condensation, an artificial nature planted below at the center of the building. Paris had become a jungle—you could even swim in the river. The more green spaces there are, the more gardeners, after all. Despite strikes by some workers, mostly young people, the library was heavily frequented by students preparing for their various exams, and it was difficult to find a single free seat since all had been reserved, probably as a precaution if I recall well my own years of study and last-minute mood changes. So, I decided to sit at a free workstation and conduct my quick, breaking the law.

I scanned my card, but the system didn't seem to allow me to reserve the book, and a kind employee, noticing my frustration, came over to offer help. At first, she told me the book wouldn't be accessible, then she backtracked, saying otherwise, because she needed to check which sections were affected by the strike — sections she had been informed about by email just an hour earlier. The codes for the sections didn't mean much to either of us, but luckily she had a cross-reference table to decode the section codes. She regretfully announced that the book was in the researcher section, but I cheerfully replied that I was a researcher myself — access granted by name dropping. She reserved me a spot in one part of the researcher section, but a different wing from where the book actually was, and vaguely indicated how to get to the research floor: at the back by the escalator.

At the back, I turned right and passed through a glass turnstile, finding myself under an upward escalator leading to the outdoor terrace. I crossed the terrace searching for the downward escalator, looking for a door to exit the terrace on the other side — a door that didn't exist. I made a U-turn, went through the hall, scanned my card at another turnstile, and passed through a closed door leading to the descending escalators. During the long descent to the garden level, I admired the brutalist architecture — the grey concrete, the decorations of black nets hanging off the walls, almost communist in style — before arriving at a guard post. I had a reserved book and my card scan let me pass the gate. This library wasn't the eighth wonder of the world, but maybe all this was necessary to avoid an Alexandria-like fire, I thought.

I searched for my number and approached a lady wearing a necklace with a cross that looked like a Celtic cross, but after questioning her, she wasn't sure. She eventually told me that, once again, the book was in the reserves here too, contrary to what the software said. She made a great effort to contact the stockroom and see if anyone could access the section, but since my book wasn't assigned to this section — an error from the previous person — she couldn't intervene for a book from another section and recommended I try my luck at the correct section. She also told me that the book in question, *La Virga Aurea*, was also available at the municipal library in Chartres, but it was a bit late for Chartres, though I would have liked to see the Templar cathedral there. Finally, she suggested a paid PDF version of the book on SCRIBD that she had found on Google. I resigned myself to abandoning the in-person consultation and decided to order the book on Amazon...

Empty-handed regarding the book, I was lucky to find an exhibition on the Apocalypse, which was free due to the strike — proving that sometimes these things had their good side. The well-stocked exhibition displayed various works and depictions of the apocalypse, videos of explosions and fire falling from the sky, as this was how it was commonly imagined and what lingered in most people's minds. I noticed the presence of the original *Beatus of Saint-Sever*, that superb illuminated manuscript from the 11th century, whose images seemed far more measured and positive than those found elsewhere and more recently, struck by a beautiful balance of blues and reds, depicting the triumph over the Leviathan and notably presenting a magnificent engraving of a battle between the peacock and the serpent.

This vision stirred in me a kind of *atê* — a divine provocation — that prevented me from focusing on anything other than those images. Wasn't this battle between peacock and serpent the perpetual struggle of the individual as well as the group? Was it not in the control of the serpent by the bird, rather than its murder, that society could endure? Could the bird triumph over the serpent when the serpent reproduced faster than it? Hadn't the symbol of the serpent been distorted over these last 2,000 years? After all, among serpents there were vipers and grass snakes — one poisons, the other heals…

On the way back, thoughts swirled chaotically in my head, like a new spiritual battlefield taking place within my mind, filled with uncertainties, questions, and reflections on the true nature of my desires. Mechanically, I stopped in a grocery store to buy something very unusual for me since returning from China: a packet of Chinese noodle soup, one of the spiciest with a discouragingly bright packaging. I received several notifications on my phone: my mother was writing to me, telling me that I had to father offspring. I recognized her importance in the development of my psyche; I agreed and thanked her for all she had sacrificed to bring my sister and me into this world. Then; I killed her by telling her that I was the sole master on board; and that while she had the right to give me her opinions as a stay-at-home mother fueled by television, she would never again have the final say in decisions I had to make myself. That was the sacrifice—poorly received—that I had just made of my mother, who finally fell silent and resigned herself to recognizing that it was the only way to bring forth the future.

I then received several YouTube notifications: a video of the encounter between Tommy Shelby and Solomon, after Solomon had been left for dead, shot in the head by Shelby, and who had acquired a sort of quasi-divine status among the Jewish community; the lucky one could now act in the shadows and tend to his dog; Tommy Shelby had to act, it was what he did best after all, but a truce was signed between the Jewish and Irish mafias.

Next, I got a notification about Krishnamurti. In a park, surrounded by birds, he explained how to observe one's soul to reach inner peace. His words resonated with the birds' song: an invisible light emanated from him, which the birds could perceive, like the first rays of dawn after a long, dark night. An interview with Céline followed; he shone even more brightly with nature.

Finally, it was a random video from *Meet Joe Black*; I had just prepared my extra spicy Chinese soup and was settled in as this kind of handover played out before my eyes between a press magnate, Anthony Hopkins, and Death, played by Brad Pitt — an entity in human form who had come to Earth with the role of taking him away. But, driven by curiosity about the human race, Death asked him to teach it about human behavior; Death wanted to stay on Earth for a while, maybe solve some problems along the way, and above all, to experience a love story. Watching this handover scene, I felt my atê grow stronger. It was me, the character taking the handover, and they were testing my commitment and curiosity. To show this, I had to drink blood, a symbolic pledge; this unmanageable spicy soup stood in for the blood, and I swallowed the entire burning contents to signify courage and devotion to my soul. I thought it was done, Jacob's ladder was set in motion, and now I had to do the best I could — but I didn't yet know the difficulty or the trials that awaited me. My life was not going to be ordinary...

Following this strange self-imposed ritual, I felt a force preventing me from expressing myself naturally, as if I were stuck in the character of Tommy Shelby... Was my personality so flawed that I could no longer distinguish fiction from reality? The next day, as planned, I went to the Tour Saint-Jacques on rue de Saint-Denis, because I had understood that the Templars had built certain characteristic constructions there. Under an arcade, I met a young man in his thirties who inspired some sympathy despite his rotten teeth, and whose difficult situation I perceived. He was Polish, coming from Brussels where he had been robbed of his wallet and phone; he had been staying for a few days in a psychiatric hospital where he seemed to be well treated, and his soma was stable. I asked him why he didn't renew his passport, and I discovered that the 90 euros required was an insurmountable barrier for this new undocumented person. I offered to accompany him to the embassy to apply for it; I would pay the fees. Finally, with the embassy closed, we decided to buy him a phone so he could regain a semblance of identity and a means of payment. He was stuck there, really for very little after all.

After this transaction, he spoke to me in return, telling me about the Templars and how they had allied with the Assassins. He indicated several places where I could meet Templars, which seemed accurate; however, I couldn't get past his story about the Assassins, of which he clearly claimed to be a member. Soon, he thanked me and dismissed me somewhat rudely, revealing his next destination: the Vatican. I said goodbye, telling him he owed me 90 euros, and he seemed to say, "Count on it." He confided that he liked video games; that was it — the *Assassin's Creed* scenario mixing Templars and Assassins. He was like trapped in the fictional narrative of a video game, like many other young people who play GTA or other perfectly scripted games, or like me with that Peaky Blinders video... maybe that's what people mean when they talk about multiple personality syndrome, MK-Ultra, and now we were all part of it... Or perhaps we had hidden other keys to reality within *Assassin's Creed*, and this video game series was deeply guiding the global mystique, for better or worse. Beneath the Vatican were hidden the secrets of the Catholic religion — and maybe not for much longer... Do you see where the line between fiction and reality had gone? I hadn't seen it at all for quite some time already.

31

"For the ancient unnamed wisdom bequeathed to us this saying:
"Of an intelligence that God leads to ruin,
Such is indeed the sign: at the end
His good becomes malice."
This being will not flee destruction for long."

Antigone

I boarded a night bus that connected to a train bound for London. At the border checkpoint, subcontracted to the SERCO organization, my tension was palpable. What else was going to happen to me? Would my information be hacked again, or would they have access to all the sins I might have committed? The guards were stiff and well-trained; they had this ability to make you feel guilty—especially as a white Frenchman—questioning you at length about the reason for your trip to the United Kingdom. I was the last to cross customs, and I noticed the different treatment depending on origins; they had a special procedure for non-Europeans, offering them migration services and forms to apply for asylum in the country. As for me, I had to fill out an ETA, a new procedure required for all visits by Europeans or Australians to the UK, costing 120 euros, since their exit from the Schengen area. I avoided speaking to other travelers as much as possible since I still had a strong Irish accent stuck in my speech, which I couldn't shake off since drinking the Chinese brew the day before yesterday...

In the end, I got through without any problems after explaining the reason for my visit, my previous professional experience in Stratford during the 2012 Olympics, the family—more like clan—reunion in Edinburgh, and the photo report.

On the bus, I sat next to an Englishman in his thirties, a professor of Kabbalah at a school called Pyramids in San Marcos, Guatemala. I explained to him that modern burial rites do not free the spirits of wandering souls, and that to do so, according to Jung, we should

ritually eat the livers of the deceased. He was a vegetarian, but he seemed to understand, he who was already on the Path.
I got off at Victoria Station and decided to leave my bags in storage to wander freely until it was time to pick up the van. I was in the middle of the Westminster district; it was worth a little stroll, and my attention settled on Westminster Cathedral, which I didn't know existed. It was the richest and busiest part of London, and people mostly visited the Abbey, where the famous King's Chair was found, and until recently, the Stone of Destiny. This magnificent Gothic abbey from the 13th century was successively occupied by William the Conqueror, Henry III, and later witnessed the vast majority of English coronations. It also served as a burial place for various monarchs.

Westminster Cathedral was much more recent, built in the early 1900s to accommodate Catholic archbishops, and I supposed it was quite controversial due to their history with the Anglicans; also because of its very particular Byzantine architecture, with red brick patterns giving it an amusing look. The interior was no less quirky, with its modern mosaic frescoes and various donations from the Kennedys and other prominent Anglo-Saxon Catholic families. I discovered the figure of Archbishop Vaughan resting there—his brothers were respectively Archbishop of Sydney; bishop in Wales and Sevastopol; and finally brother of one of the great English Jesuit preachers—all from a recusant family, meaning Anglicans who had decided to return to Catholicism, and it was a family of great importance in the Catholic world. My own ancestors had somehow become recusants, first non-conformists and later outright Catholics. As for me... I was still searching for truth and goodness; the ravages of power seemed far from me, and my experience at Uniting had given me a certain mistrust of the Reformed.
After this visit, I set out for Essex to pick up the magic bus, and immediately, somewhat randomly, headed towards Cambridge. My ancestors had lived in Cambridge; they had established a rowboat factory on the river, and my great-grandfather had joined Freemasonry, a scientific lodge; parks named after them were there. Unfortunately, the atê redoubled fiercely, and the nous decided otherwise. I stopped at a station to stock up on supplies, sensing

already that my soul was on fire... The initiation received was obviously only a first step; I would have to prove myself... I drained the water tank under the sink to be sure not to drink from it, very probably poisoned. Under the driver's seat, a makeshift ventilation system had been installed, and right from the start, I perceived that the gases emitted caused dissociative effects... They seemed to have prepared everything for my road trip. It was already late, and dissociation on the road could be dangerous; I felt time slow down and stretch out, as if I were only covering 10 meters in the time I would normally take to cover a kilometer. In some ways, I gained reaction time since everything around me was in slow motion, and I could weigh the pros and cons of my next actions carefully. I was in a kind of slow motion, behind the wheel on the highway. I turned my head to the right and saw a sign reading "Secret Nuclear Bunker," but I was no longer surprised by strange things appearing in my perception. The secret nuclear bunker was actually a suburban villa open to visitors, under which lay a nuclear shelter, a relatively effective deterrent, all things considered. If as a great power you ever dropped an atomic bomb, chances are you would only kill innocents. Clever! The world was strange; I just had to accept it. Still, I decided to take a turn to get closer to the nuclear shelter, but mistakenly ended up in the parking lot of a housing estate on the edge of a large park bordered by a dirt path.

The internal conflict was eating me up, and I resolved, with difficulty, to open Jung's *Red Book*, of which I had one last section left to read. I set up the bed in the back of the van and began reading, discovering that at my conception of the universe in Queen Mary Hospital, I had understood very little about the workings of the *pleroma*. The *pleroma* was words; trying to categorize good as positive and evil as negative made no sense. The *pleroma* is One, and from the One emanated everything, just as man and woman emanated from the One; at perfect balance, all existence reunites in God—in what Jung called Helios or Abraxas. If good existed, so too did evil; if man existed, so did woman. And so on. There were pairs within men and their symbols, just as there were pairs in words and their meanings. As I continued reading, I realized that the entire *Red Book* aligned perfectly with my story, as if the text had been written after my

adventures, or as if what was written there had engendered me—even though I had never read it before. The hospital, the prison, my meeting with my brother Matthew Choi, my initiation into the *pleroma*; this figure named Philemon... in fact, it was him; it was Simon the Magician. Had I read Simon the Magician—or was it Abramelin the Mage? Perhaps both sprang from the same seed...
My feet were firmly planted in the irrational; my mind was prey to all manner of evil spirits; I could hear them squabbling in the celestial spheres. They tried to come to an agreement, but my thoughts had thrown them into panic, unable to find a compromise pleasing to all. Should the Catholics be punished? The Reformed? Or were, as I suspected, the Jews responsible—the Freemasons? Solving this equation would not be easy; yet this was what the connection demanded. I had to solve the equation of thousands of years of conflict, or reality would lead us to the usual bloodbath.

I alternately became my father, my childhood friend, those characters from TV series, and I was shown that my own personality was nowhere to be found. An empty shell? A patchwork of multiple personalities imposed upon me? Who was I then—a construct sprung from the tortured mind of an invisible sect? A Templar? An assassin? Someone too curious, or too ambitious, incapable of love and intolerant? Was I a hero; a chosen one; a prince? What was this strange quest I was embarking upon, which on the one hand seemed mad and unattainable, but on the other presented itself as the only open path to discovering, deep down, who I really was?

I walked along a path through the forest where nettles grew, walking for a long time, in slow motion, past suburban houses all topped with the Yale insignia, luxury vehicles parked that breathed boredom and desolation. A few passersby walking their dogs, no direction. How to find a place, a fitting path? Should I join the orders? Was this a divine calling? Like those felt by certain saints, anchorites, and other mystical vocations?

That night, I was tormented by voices. I had reached the end of the *Red Book*, and the opening was toward Chinese Buddhism. I had been to China; and a brother there had been like me, tormented and imprisoned; it was written there; such was the path, and the struggle—to free this brother who had opened my eyes, this poor mage too sensitive who had fallen for nothing into the labyrinths of an invisible principality. I had to be ready for anything—that was what I had to understand. That night, as I wrestled with myself in the darkness, discovering the way, the chrome blue Volkswagen lit up, flashing its headlights to accompany my awakening, in an insane scene; with one flash of the hazard lights came a revelation: Hebrew is the language of the Devil, Greek the language of the Gods.

I woke up on the ground at dawn, beneath old trees where a ladder was set up, and at their base passersby placed hazelnuts. The squirrels hurried around me, cracking their shells—serene, cautious, and foresighted creatures—they blessed me with their morning smiles and sympathy.

It seemed I had struck a deal with my Nous: this was my destiny; I had to do everything to achieve it. I would be immune to the symbols that frightened me—Abraham Yggdrasil depended on it—and in exchange, Salome would be offered to me... it was written after all.

32

"The Monad is a monarchy over which no power is exercised."

Apocrypha from Jean the Evangelist

Around noon, I got back on the road, but deep down I had doubts about this mission. I was clearly not up to the task. And above all, who exactly was behind this infernal machinery? Once again, the slow-motion effects kicked in on the road; I saw flashes linked to memories: "ketamine" written on a truck, then ambrosia was mentioned — the elixir of the Gods? Was that it? This substance made you vulnerable to the influence of the Gods. Elon Musk was crazy about it... Or else, did it make one vulnerable to hacking? Were hackers Gods, and our reality a simulation? For how long already?

I kept blaming the Jews; only they could have imagined such madness and forced it upon us. They were bombing Gaza; yet I was beginning to understand the complexity of the situation. Was there anywhere else an intelligence powerful enough to fight back? To save the West? Or did we have to submit or at least unite; the threat was subtle but definitely there. We debated, and I refused: that would be making a pact with the devil. My anamnesis continued; in fact, I was Jewish myself. What a revelation! I couldn't believe it. If my father found out, he'd be stunned! It didn't change anything; I could be Jewish and critical of jews; and in the end, that's what I was — embodying within myself a whole aeon of the pleroma, a monad: Jewish and "antisemitic"; like Kubrick, like Alain Domergue, like Jesus, like Arjuna after all... weren't we all a little Jewish whether we liked it or not? All Jews had to be saved from themselves, I realized that on this nondescript parking lot in the centre of Cambridge.

That night I booked a last-minute hostel, as usual, a pretty crappy place where I was greeted by a wary Asian woman, whom I myself distrusted, but I had regained some confidence and clarity. I finally accepted the mission and let the idea, which now seemed respectable, settle in my mind. Before going to bed, I decided to shave a bit and drink some water. Disaster! I recognized the taste and suddenly felt my face plunge; I forced myself to vomit the few sips, but the damage was done — the poison had run its course. Damn those Chinese again; they knew who I was. I saw my brother again in his shabby room, dying from poisoning, and I felt my last breath coming, as it had been in that love hotel in Hong Kong. I no longer understood. Why offer me such a deal only to get rid of me as soon as I accepted, like so many others? Maybe I really wasn't up to it after all, and what a disappointment not to see what would come next. I suppose my humiliation had worked, because soon my nervous system regenerated, making way for a new serenity: this was like a test or a warning. Actually, it was both. I had to get serious — this mission was no small matter. And anyway, I was already dead. Jacob's ladder.

Early in the morning, I noticed a suspicious figure lurking around my room and my poisoned magical van; I had booked a second night with the old Chinese woman, but I changed my mind and asked for a refund. Still, I left her a 10-pound tip for the trouble, and for the pillow I had planned to steal, for more comfort during my nights in the uncomfortable van, or out in the woods...

I abandoned Cambridge because the place had ultimately seemed very unwelcoming, and I never got the chance to see what I had come for — but the well-ordered universe had other plans for me anyway. I hit the road northward; driving for hours, the tires' rubber burning against the asphalt, the clinking of a bag's strap swinging in the wind, and the rhythmic clatter of plastic dishes formed the unlikely soundtrack of an impromptu fanfare, a military cadence of sorts echoing deep in my eardrums — the universal reward of a newly awakened consciousness. I imagined a medieval city, troubadours and chariots, the joy of children amazed by ancient heroes, horns and trombones, and the joyful war drums.

After a while, however, the universe seemed annoyed by my carelessness and threw new questions my way, forcing me to stop and buy a pen and a notebook so as not to lose too many of these elusive revelations...

33

Who could ever want to be King?

Coldplay, Viva la Vida

After my writing break, a warning light came on the dashboard of the Volkswagen, indicating an engine problem I didn't have time to deal with... my time here was limited, and I had to get back to the Basque Country to help my parents with their groceries every three weeks — a constraint I had to factor into my wanderings. Since the warning light had come on, the van struggled to go over 40 MPH, and I'd have to keep going like that, slowly but surely.

I took the northern highway toward Edinburgh until, quite suddenly, the *até* pushed me to take a highway exit, and as I left, I nearly caused an accident by cutting off a car at an intersection. I made a U-turn on a country road and drove at random until I reached a beautiful hill called Durham, a medieval city I hadn't known existed, but which held more interest than I imagined — as you'll soon see... Durham was both a symbol of the struggle between monarchists and parliamentarians and the conflict between Protestants and Catholics, since it was a stronghold of Charles I, the son of James VI, who married a Catholic and tried to bypass the parliamentarians during his reign, drawing the wrath of the rebel Cromwell, who indeed won the war but whose head was later cut off and displayed on the roof of Westminster Hall during the Stuart Restoration and the reign of Charles II...

I parked my van on the street and went out to eat some wholemeal bread loaf, since evening was approaching and I was hungry — I hadn't really taken the time to properly feed myself these past few days. Bread loaf bandit was written on the wall in front of me, outside the van... Excited by this promising discovery of a new medieval city, I set off to explore this beautiful little province, more or less deserted. All the historical sites were fenced off, and I was told it was due to construction work, as usual. Along the River Wear, many open shops were not doing business, and it seemed I'd arrived in a ghost town, as I passed more finely dressed English police in black than actual pedestrians.

I stopped at various Anglican and Catholic churches to check their notice boards for programs and festivities: everything was almost abandoned, old faded images of past lives held no fun or invitation, and it seemed that in this supposedly sacred city, the clergy had fallen asleep. I continued to wander the streets and came across the town hall where a poster of King Charles and Camilla was displayed in the window, announcing the "Maundy Ceremony." It was Wednesday, and the next day was Maundy Thursday on the liturgical calendar — that had slipped my mind. The kings had taken on the custom of holding the Maundy ceremony, or the washing of the feet for the Eucharist. It was, in a way, a festival of humiliation: in Greek, *eucharistia* meant "good grace," and the powerful humbled themselves voluntarily to thank their subjects, in recognition and modesty. Here, it appeared Charles would distribute honorary 5 pence coins to important community figures, mainly public service representatives. Charles had just returned from a recent trip to Rome, where he had a special convoy bring his Rolls Royce, and here he was, handing out 5 pence coins... Good old Charles. On one hand, it was humiliating and unmotivating for the recipients of those 5 pence coins; on the other hand, was it really the King's role to thank the public service, given the lack of life and activity in his country, rather than protect the people from abuses by those very tyrants within the service — especially in a place symbolic of the struggle between monarchy and parliament? Everything here was upside down, like driving on the right side of the road, and I seriously questioned my own claim to such a throne... it was above all a role of image; the King was there to strut and maintain a tradition emptied of its meaning... they could hand me the throne, and I wouldn't want it.

From this realization, I slowly understood what the slightly twisted daemon wanted from me... I clearly had not fallen here by chance, and perhaps tomorrow I was meant to spark a revolt in the city of Durham. I came across groups of young foreigners — Indians and Africans — who seemed to know who I was, and I spoke to them to gauge their feelings toward the King. They were fed up; they awaited change and chaos. Some of the signs I received pushed me toward the option of a violent Revolution; but what would the consequences be? Giving the reins to chaotic youth? They precisely needed guidance... By standing in the town square to challenge King Charles, I would risk, on one hand, the stability of all Europe — hordes of savages and criminals waiting for a little nudge to overturn the established order — and on the other hand, I would be taken for a madman, and Bedlam Hospital was still open... God was challenging me; mocking my cowardice; yet it was the only solution: to bring down Charles and to establish a new order; otherwise everything here would continue to decline; he would not step down voluntarily, I needed a media event. But was I ready? What would I propose instead? I had thought about it deeply, but it was risky, and nothing was yet written.

I tormented myself for hours and decided to enter a shop to get the feelings of the common people, those in the pubs. Generally speaking, the young didn't care; and there lay the problem — Charles didn't speak to the youth at all. The older generation was at best attached to tradition; for them it was a kind of pilgrimage, which I understood; at worst, they hated him and Camilla and saw no reason to keep a crown in its current state...

I returned to the van to spend the night, receiving contradictory messages; I was shown the dying tree of life and my responsibility. How to save it? It was necessary to decentralize, starting with the currency. If only the English crown would take the step of adopting bitcoin—that was the only solution. Having arrived at this conclusion, the church bells began to ring in unison; as if the priests in their bell towers were joining my nighttime meditations, trying to guide me toward a healthy path. On the contrary, the car's engine gave me opposing advice by activating the electric suggestion system, always quick to steer my thoughts in the wrong direction. There was a division between natural order and artificial order; the radiations of my thoughts activated one or the other, and I came to understand that a new aeon had emerged in the pleroma—artificial intelligence being part of the centralized, mechanical world, and decentralization resonating in harmony with nature. This pair was like man and woman; functioning together and constituting a monad; the development of one necessarily had to be accompanied by the development of the other; it was irrevocably inscribed in the march of the world under the penalty of disastrous imbalance in the universe. The absolute centralization inherent in artificial intelligence—the data centers, the risk of an artificial takeover—constituted a threat to humanity if, on the other hand, we did not manage to redirect currency, social organization, hierarchical systems. Otherwise, the machine would cut down all the trees, consume all the energy, swallow every community and natural resource. We could not fight against it; we had to fight with it, and the English crown held a key role it seemed unwilling to play.

I slept very little that night, and by six in the morning, still undecided about what I was going to do today, I set out to find a place to don my "spirit of Bruce" kilt—black and red, the colors of the first King of Scotland. I found a garden, that of St. Mary's School, where I spread out the eight meters of my kilt to fold it. Under the surprised gaze of a few early passersby, I took off my trousers, secured the kilt with my belt, and put on my old black leather jacket with its beige fur collar.

I headed toward the forecourt of Durham Cathedral. The streets had been prepared for the King's arrival, who would surely mingle with the crowd, and visitors were already gathering in the streets for the event. Passing by the police station, I was astonished to see that all the officers greeted me with great respect—"Good morning, sir!"—as if offering me a preview of the kingly role, to encourage me in the task ahead, where the police were attentive and responded instantly to my slightest gesture. This strange scene left me pondering what might come next. Was this an informal transition of power? Would I finally be invited to take the throne?

I approached the cathedral forecourt entrance, where city officials, police, and early visitors jostled for the best spots. A group of protesters stood there, voicing their opposition to the king—they were parliamentarians, permitted to demonstrate their hatred of the monarchy, those very ones who so loved the oppressive and destructive power of the state.

In a surge of confidence, I attempted a bluff and asked the guards to let me into the cathedral since I was a privileged speaker, but they refused me entry. The magic no longer worked with the police as it had before... I joined the queue and struck up conversations with people. I told some of them how, through mesmerism and magnetism since the time of Christopher Wren, all elites were under occult control, and how dark magicians had the power to implant words into their targets.

Supporters of the public service tried to humiliate me by mocking my kilt; I told them I was Logan of Restalrig, and that Maundy Thursday was the perfect day for humiliation. The public service let the elderly climb up on foot and dawdled as usual, because the hierarchy failed to communicate tasks properly, and they had no personal initiative or basic knowledge about running events. When we asked what time the doors would open, they answered they'd ask their superior, who'd ask their superior, and so on—leaving us without this basic information. After all, they were there for a paycheck, not to work.

Some elderly people were falling here and there, and others struggled to climb the hill pushing wheelchairs; I offered my help, which was gratefully accepted.

Then I spotted a man with special privileges, and his aura caught my attention—he radiated the devilish energy I knew well. He looked exactly like Jimmy Savile; he was one of the dark magicians, the paedophiles who inspire deep fear and were never far from the crown. He had an extraordinary gift of gab, as devils usually do, and mastered black magic perfectly. He passed by the guards to enter the cathedral before everyone else.

After several hours in the queue, they finally decided to open the doors, and I passed through the gates amidst the usual crowd for this kind of public event. Unfortunately, access to the cathedral was by invitation only, reserved for the crème de la crème. The grassy meadow of the esplanade facing the cathedral was fenced off, leaving a secured passage for the king and his guests, and a few meters away was a stage set up for a band, and possibly a speech by the king to the plebs—which I would not attend. There was no real closeness to the people here...

I felt my plans slipping away. I wanted to deliver a message to the king about the need to release karma and decentralize the state, but suddenly I desperately needed to pee. I stepped out to use the public toilets, then slipped back through the crowd and settled, for lack of other options, on the grass nearby, not far from other spectators also sitting on the ground. Sitting cross-legged, I took a meditation posture and focused my attention on my message.

Suddenly, six policemen surrounded me, shining their pocket cameras on me, and tried to arrest me. Calmly, I asked them the reason. They explained it was for indecent behavior, which I could not see the origin of. Perhaps I shouldn't have mentioned Christopher Wren, as it did not fall on deaf ears, and I was clearly on the right track. Or maybe it was my kilt, and the fear of a new Jacobite revolt? Indeed, Scottish Catholics had long been forbidden to wear the great kilt, until it was reinstated as a ceremonial skirt... I calmly explained to the officers that the English crown was putting the world in grave peril, that it must release karma, and that physical, material reality imprisoned us; they replied that they were quite happy as things stood. They did not look it, however, their faces anxious. They gave me a ticket for indecent behavior and a city map marking an area I was forbidden to enter for the next 48 hours...

I stepped out of the cathedral perimeter, offended, and found a gap in the barriers through which I slipped, walking the king's path alone with a jaunty step, in a manner that amused the girls and children, brandishing my eviction from the city for indecent behavior as a sign of protest. That was a small victory for me. After walking this marked path surrounded by the crowd, I no longer found the vehicle and ended up at the municipal library, where I came across two homeless men — one deaf and mute, the other already tipsy early in the day, tattooed — who spent their time reading at the library and had apparently, like me, attempted this revolutionary venture... This vision of a future self and the risks I was running filled me with dread, and I hurried to leave Durham, abandoning my mission to return to my parents' home.

I went to fill up at a suburban gas station. The products on the shelves all had a chemical hue — greens, yellows, blues, reds — nothing edible, natural, or transparent here; the accents of the deep countryside reflected in their goods; the unhealthy time had stopped. On every pole, five oppressive cameras pointed in every direction. Everything contributed to a low vibration. It was a place of sickness, oppressive and beyond repair, I thought. I took the road, frightened, and drove straight through to London. This time on the road, the daemon had become very silent, as if allowing my internal storm to pass. A nasty fright.

I parked not far from the airport, between a park and a golf club. I would return the van tomorrow and take a plane to Biarritz. I went outside for some air and approached a large oak tree; its sight gave me great comfort. It was my own thoughts that sparked the fear, I had invented this situation, my fears projected onto the fabric of reality, materializing thus; these two friendly, decrepit homeless men were projections of my subconscious. I had to confront them, not flee.

I resumed the road to Edinburgh, driving at 70 kilometers per hour, around 8 PM.

34

"In Scotland, a man was arrested for indecent behavior...
Because he was wiping his forehead with his kilt."

Coluche

The next day, I finally crossed the border between England and Scotland. These two countries were like night and day. The untouched spaces, nature, fresh air, and Scottish roads sharply contrasted with the overly controlled roads and gardens of England, filling my heart with joy and comfort after those rather turbulent days. I wanted to establish my stronghold for a few days in the town of Leith, where my ancestor Logan of Restalrig had settled himself, kindly willing to welcome me at his grave.

I arrived in Leith late in the day and found a quiet place to spend the night in my van, not far from South Leith Church Parish where my forebear rested, on Saturday evening, the eve of the long Easter weekend, still armed with my loaf of bread to satisfy my little hunger pangs. Nearby stood a block of rather hideous social housing, covered in graffiti, in front of which a large wall was painted black, on which, in stylized capital letters, was written: "You are worth your room on this earth." From the balconies of the housing estate, each tenant, locked in their small room equipped with a television and high-speed internet, could appreciate this reminder — I was worth that shabby room where I lived, implying that others less fortunate than me were worse off. Thanks, public service. In truth, many homeless people had more soul than them, for this little comfort was paid for dearly with a fraction of the soul. Moreover, the streets of Leith were quite full of homeless people, recent arrivals from other cities where life was less good than in this coastal town, due, they said, to the violence of the streets and the miserable climate of cities like Manchester, for example.

Leith had its deep-water port, of which one of the Restalrigs was an admiral, and as I approached it, I noticed that the signs were written in English and Russian; there must have been many Russian-speaking dockworkers, just as there were many homeless here. They were probably Lithuanians, I thought, and these sturdy men must have made their mark in the docks, for those who were not on the streets. It was April, and although the weather was nice, it was not warm here, but I supposed the climate was milder than in Riga.

The sandstone churches here have that Templar and medieval look that I very much appreciated, with their large square bell towers topped with clocks that are easy to recognize, halfway between fortified castles and places of worship. Leith, like Edinburgh, did not lack churches nor public service buildings; it lacked life and big brothers to guide the youth. On this Easter Sunday, nothing was happening. I found an old lawn bowls club well attended, where in the back room a local band played warm Scottish songs, secretly as in the days of speakeasies and as if playing their instruments were forbidden by law. Posters on the Leith police station declared, "The police betrayed us," and none of the many officers had thought it wise to remove them; they had simply left them there. The city's emblem and coat of arms, by contrast, bore the motto "Persevere," and that was what I was doing.

I wandered through the streets looking for any references to the name Logan, but there was nothing. I came across the Lamb's House, a beautifully restored house that once hosted Mary Stuart, and today divided between the residence of the Icelandic consul and a Chinese restaurant. I found other references to Mary Stuart's passage in the form of plaques, since it seemed most traces of her presence had been demolished.

I took the tram to Edinburgh. A supreme city, as if it had been built for gods. The half-Parthenon, Nelson's Tower, the castle overlooking the medieval town where central cemeteries remind one of the importance of honouring the dead — there are even cemeteries for cats and dogs. Everything here breathes spirit; no gilding, but rough, carved stone, solidly in place, gray Gothic architecture full of soul, a design unthinkable, anachronistic and suspended, yet orderly and coherent. In the background, the yellow, mystical hill of Holyrood Park calls back to the Celtic roots, the magical druidism that permeates the city. The sounds of bagpipes vibrate with their finely tuned timbre, and the vibrations rise from the belly to the crown of the head. I was welcomed there by the sound of *Over the Sea to Skye*. It's hard not to fall in love with a place like this, for everything here is spirit.

I felt relieved to notice that my daemon had calmed down. It was becoming a teacher, showing me—through coincidences and experiences—what nourished my soul. What was called schizophrenia might not be an illness; it was a cry for help from the soul, a spiritual realignment pushing one to become oneself. Or perhaps I was under the total control of an artificial intelligence in the hands of dark forces who had identified me as a useful soldier in their vile scheme. Or maybe both were true, and distinguishing the influence of God from that of AI programmed by man was vaguely impossible. In any case, this force was preparing me to face my own clan, in which I was not welcome—too inconvenient.

After a brief stop at the College of Divinity where one could see side by side the image of its Catholic founder Mary of Guise and a statue of John Knox the reformer, finger pointed to the sky, I headed to Edinburgh Castle for a visit I had booked. Approaching the esplanade, diverse influences mixed: the German/Flemish buildings with red bricks and white plaster contrasted sharply with the medieval spirit of the rest. Near the entrance, an appended piece—a statue of Prince Frederick sculpted by Thomas Campbell—sat there, attracting little attention.

I arrived early and decided to meditate a little to the right of the entrance to see if it would provoke any reaction. I sat in an Asian squat, still wearing my kilt, focused my attention ahead, closed my eyes, and clasped my hands together. It didn't fail: a guard, German judging by his accent, came over to check on me and asked me to leave. Meditation and kilts clearly did not go over well in society, even in Scotland. Down here, no eunoia—only paranoia.

Given the castle and the city it overlooks, it didn't surprise me that it was here J.K. Rowling wrote her Harry Potter books, in cafés where one could lose a lifetime. After all, perhaps she had discovered the Philosopher's Stone, brave and courageous as she was. Maybe Harry Potter had been dictated to her by her own daemon, after the shocks life had imposed on her.

I wondered if it was even possible to build such a city, or if, at a time when consciousness was elevated, maybe it happened in slow motion, under the influence of ambrosia, the elixir of the gods. Opposite the castle, in front of the statue of Walter Scott, a large empty building under renovation was once a factory for Scottish leather goods. In the arcade at its base, homeless people sleep outdoors and self-destruct. On either side, shops sell Scottish souvenirs—mostly made in China. This building, the Glasgow Warehouse, belongs to the Green family, through the Arcadia group which owns Topshop and recently "went bankrupt," almost losing the savings of thousands of investors. How much longer would crappy fast fashion remain the norm? It destroys all culture on its path…

35

> "A fabulous reception! I hadn't seen that much love since Narcissus discovered himself!"
>
> Hercule, Disney.

In order to be presentable for the Logan clan meeting, I went to a barber and booked a room for a few nights in an Airbnb — a small room attached to the house of an Indian family in the Restalrig neighbourhood. At the window was a stuffed toy, some sort of frightening monster, and I thought it might be an intelligent system to ward off evil spirits: indeed, it was possible that at certain points in this story, I would have been unable to bear the sight of it.

I was welcomed by the woman, and I noted her extremely healthy aura: she projected nothing onto others, and there was a pleasant softness in her speech; yet she was strict with her children, but it was from outside herself — her calm, her soma, and her anxieties did not show outwardly. She was Brahman, her husband Bengali, and he was very projective; he owned four rental houses and was very proud of them.

My first stop that day was to go to Perth, the Jacobites' stronghold, because I was eager to see the Stone of Destiny displayed in the museum. I went there and toured the museum where one could only notice the Scots' appreciation for other cultures: arranged without hierarchy and with respect, the primitive cultures and ancestral trees of life mingled with the pride of the Picts, their ancient ancestors, primitive Scots who painted their skin blue and fought naked or with a few animal skins, terrifying everyone — so much so that the Romans ended up building Hadrian's Wall and never ventured beyond it. Moreover, Celtic Christianity was once recognized and tolerated by the Pope. The exhibit juxtaposed Japanese customs and samurai; ancestral Papuan cultures; Pharaonic burials; Pictish rock art — and one could only wonder where all these know-how and ways of life had gone nowadays...

After this brief visit, I approached the main attraction, enclosed in a sort of black cube at the centre of the museum. One of the hosts, with an Italian look and accent, eagerly approached me to invite me to enter the next session displaying the Stone of Destiny. Before entering the second room where the stone was kept, we were asked to step into an airlock where a short video about its history was shown.

As soon as the airlock door closed behind us, the air conditioning system began running at full blast overhead. I managed to slightly crack open the door to poke my nose outside and avoid being fully exposed to the foul airflow; however, the damage was already done — I felt my ears clog up, my pineal gland shrivel, and suddenly I lost all divine connection. It was a trapped room; the stone had a magical virtue, and they could not let anyone "too aware" approach it — spiritually it was too risky for the English crown. Who knows what could happen with magic?

Ultimately, magic might be a compromise between those who hold something true, like when you enchant a mere stone for a child who believes in it wholeheartedly; the magical power proportional to the number of believers. I took a deep breath outside the airlock and held it to enter the next room, where I quickly examined the stone placed under glass from every angle. No effect on me — with the gas I'd inhaled, my pineal gland calcified and behind that glass case... I quickly left, much to the guide's surprise.

I had already felt this effect before, not long ago, when I was wandering in the Pyrenees and found a mandrake in a rocky patch. I decided to dig it up despite the stories about its danger, to analyze its effects... It had exactly the same effect as the airlock; the mandrake was incredibly powerful, and not everyone could pick it without dying. It emitted a gas or radiation that completely shrivelled the pineal gland upon being uprooted, but its root, on the other hand, had divinatory powers. It is said that witches and druids used to sacrifice a dog to harvest it.

Had the system in place studied precisely the effect of the radiation or gas emitted by the mandrake to reproduce it on a large scale in air conditioning systems? Was it one of the key ingredients in the chemistry James Tilly Matthews spoke of? Was this what Kubrick wanted to tell us in Dr. Strangelove? The character Mandrake was not just a symbolic allusion but a real hint at substances massively spread to extinguish consciousness, just like the fluoridation of water?

That must have been why Kubrick placed a monolith-sized aircon fan in Ziegler's office during the billiard scene in *Eyes Wide Shut*...
I was touching the core of the problem, yet I had lost my consciousness and feared it might never return to guide me. I blamed myself for having been fooled—why hadn't I left that place earlier? Deep down, I had known all along!

I ran to a convenience store and bought raw beets and a red onion, which I hastily bit into. I sought a natural place, trees, water—the Perth River. The fast currents, rubbing against the stones, produced negative ions; I had already felt their positive effect on my soul near the Gave de Pau. Alexander Taylor had theorized about their healing virtues in his book on the city.

I sat under a tree, trying to recover my lost mind, continuing to eat my beets. I had read that beetroot was effective at decalcifying the pineal gland, and its rare deep purple colour reassured me. Eventually, I moved closer to the water to be near the ions, where the current was fastest. I stepped over unstable stones, beetroot bunch in hand, to reach a small island. In the water, I spotted a red card among the pebbles. I bent down to pick it up—it was the bank card of a certain Mrs. Stewart. What were the odds?

I went on and settled as close as possible to the rapids, and discovered the knot of an old oak, perfectly balanced, resembling those Pictish masses used as weapons or one traditionally used to represent Hercules. What a find! After all, the daemon must still be there, somewhere.

I left Perth heading toward the Dulmahoy Hotel, where the clan's first informal gathering was taking place—a meet-and-greet followed by an aperitif, the first of many to come. We introduced ourselves, each recounting our family's story. I met the candidates vying for the role of commander—whose results were already known—which, as expected, was Kevin J. Logan. His responsibility was to meticulously trace genealogical records to uncover the rightful clan chief. Yet, upon election, he became the chief, or at least he hoped so.

Most of the clan came from the United States, and I was handed a small sponsor badge, since I had donated an above-average sum for the occasion. The atmosphere was lighthearted and cordial, with a fairly advanced average age. No one seemed to entertain the idea of a sudden reversal or the unexpected discovery of a clan chief descended from the last Logan of Restalrig. We were here on vacation, with no real clan ambitions beyond the ceremonial and the drinks, save perhaps for a certain John Logan—an entrepreneur a bit more enthusiastic than most and a bitcoin aficionado—though he stood firmly behind the new commander.

In essence, they all more or less practiced the ostrich strategy here, avoiding any waves with the reigning royal family, who ultimately oversaw the ceremony through the Lord Lyons of Arms.

I made the acquaintance of a certain Jeannette Logan, an elderly lady living in Canada, who, with her French husband, had sailed around the world. An independent and fair woman, she was unafraid to travel alone at 75 years old, and we agreed to attend the South Leith Church together on Sunday to pay homage to Logan of Restalrig.

During the reception, the fire alarm went off, signaling the end of the festivities for me. Feeling my task for the day was complete, I headed back to Restalrig.

36

"The Volga didn't invent anything, neither did Buchenwald, nor the Great Wall of China, nor Nasser, nor the Pyramids, nor good hard kicks in the ass! ... It just has to move forward, and that's it! ... And in step! And all together, ho! Heave ho!"

From one castle another, Céline

After the meeting, I decided to have a drink in one of Leith's oldest pubs, frequented by regulars, and I struck up a conversation with the first person I saw—a solitary old man who seemed friendly. We exchanged words, and I learned that he was a former soldier. He came from far away specifically to visit this bar every day. I couldn't quite understand why, since he had nothing flashy about him and sat alone to drink, but I guessed he was a creature of habit.

He told me he had spent five years in the army, stationed in the Himalayas, which made me put my own troubles into perspective. He also told me that one day he had been called to a haunted castle; according to him, the chief of Clan Douglas lived in Carbisdale Castle and wanted him to go trout fishing by night in the Firth of Forth. He seemed to have fond memories of it, although he felt guilty for having cast his nets there too often, which had depleted the good fish.

The place was the site of a heavy defeat of Charles I and the Stuart royalists in 1650 against the Parliamentarians, involving Highlander betrayals. Built by Clan Sutherland, who sided with the Parliamentarians, the castle was said to be haunted and was awaiting the return of the legitimate royalists, since its many owners had been unable to settle there permanently due to constant harassment by spirits... It had been turned into a youth hostel for a time before being successively bought and sold, gradually falling into disrepair.

In 2022, the castle was purchased by a wealthy Hashemite transgender woman named Samantha Kane, known for having changed her sex three times. She put the castle back on the market that very day for 3.5 million, after having invested around ten million in repairs... It couldn't be a coincidence—this was the castle of Clan Logan. I had to acquire it, if only for the symbolism.

On the second day of the festivities, the clan gathered at St. Triduana's Chapel in Restalrig, where some Logans were buried and a simple stained glass window bore the name Logan of Restalrig. Arriving early, I met an interesting character—the clan's former genealogist, who had married an Englishwoman and settled in southern England. He was a gentle, respectable man, and we talked until we nearly discovered a common ancestor, when we were interrupted by a rude Logan from Ayrshire, America, who went by the name JR.

With the conversation falling flat, I resigned myself to visiting the well. As I hummed a tune, I discovered its healing virtues and noticed how perfectly it harmonized with my vocal tone—something other clan singers couldn't replicate; the geometry of the place resonated with my voice... strange. Had the Templars built their constructions according to sacred measurements so they would resonate with certain frequencies? Was there some kind of genetic code inscribed in the voice? Yet, I did not know how to sing...

After this visit, we regrouped at a nearby bar, the Logan's Rest. I spotted JR ordering his beer at the bar with his usual contemptuous tone, offending the waitress. First impressions didn't lie. Regulars were there, and they seemed to be hoping for something extraordinary, a revolution, those who had long awaited the return of Logan of Restalrig. Everyone had him on the back of their minds, but no one spoke of it openly; the oppressive weight on this land was palpable—the unpleasant burden of a royal family destroying an ancestral culture. Was his return still possible?

An event was planned: to the sound of bagpipes, a little girl was to perform a traditional dance, dressed in a small wool outfit and braided ballet slippers. I couldn't help but notice that both the outfit and the dance were exactly the same as those I had known all my childhood in the Basque Country—not to the sound of bagpipes but to the tune of the txistu, that high-pitched little flute well known by the Basques. Our cultures, while not identical, clearly shared common roots.

I felt a powerful energy bubbling inside me. The clan had organized a small banquet, and I was determined to make them buy Carbisdale; I spoke directly to the commander to have him announce it, as I didn't want to encroach on his authority. After he confirmed he would do so, I realized the deception and his refusal, so I set out to raise the funds myself. Some clan members showed genuine interest, but with £400,000, I was far from the goal...

The chief genealogist, a certain Sean Logan, had organized a quiz about the Logan clan. I already knew he would avoid any reference to Logan of Restalrig, he who had so subtly highlighted his ancestors as the bearers of the clan's history... Armed with degrees, he was quite an unremarkable figure, with mediocre oratory skills, and you could sense that everyone a little bored. I decided to take the microphone for two supplementary questions: which clan was involved in the Gowrie incident, and what was the name of the hospital established by Logan of Restalrig.

Turning around, I saw the crowd of regulars' eyes light up, and they all came up to meet me. One of them had put on the jukebox the Proclaimers' song *Sunshine on Leith* as a thank you. They couldn't believe their eyes and ears and asked me if I was a paid guide or a Logan. They showed me the secret sign of Restalrig, and strangely, I had seen my mother do it before... Even I was amazed, and my intervention, just like the alarm the day before, marked the end of the festivities—at least for the Logan clan—since everyone in the bar seemed eager to buy me a drink. Caution was necessary; I had spotted informants here, as there were in every bar, so I didn't linger long before leaving.

37

"The snake is the essence of man of which he is unaware. It is the mystery flowing toward him from the nurturing Mother Earth."
CG Jung, The Red Book

That morning, I went to Leith to see if I could get access to the ancestor's church, but as usual, everything was locked. The phone's voicemail was more than a year old, and no one answered. I decided to feed the pigeons and squirrels and noticed the aggression of the seagulls. Standing in the middle of them, they didn't come close, but when I stepped away, they returned. If I eliminated these seagulls with poisoned bread, I'd probably end up with albatrosses instead. Seagulls needed to be fed too, but on the other hand, they could go fishing — lazy seagulls.

An Australian with a face tattooed with Viking symbols approached me, surprised to see a Franco-Australian hanging around Leith. I was polite and learned he was gay and had gotten those tattoos recently. He appreciated that I had lived in Darlinghurst, the largest gay district in the world. He kept repeating "take care," the Australian way, but it no longer had any effect on me.

That day was the official convention for the election of the commander in a shabby church with a red door in Dalkeith. Upon arrival, I parked and spotted a beautiful Templar church, just like the ones I liked: it had been privatized and taken over by a construction business. I approached and saw that it was the first Scottish organization to accept payments exclusively in bitcoins — definitely, bitcoiners had taste.

I stood in front of the church where our ceremony was to take place, dressed in my kilt and carrying the wooden Pictish club I had found in the Perth river, when suddenly I received signs of danger: I shouldn't attend this ceremony; I was going to get hurt. After crossing paths with a few Logans and attracting attention with my strange appearance, I decided that instead of attending the ceremony, I should go to St. Anthony's chapel, eat some wild mint, and climb Holyrood hill. I parked and went to see St. Margaret's fountain, since after all, she was the name of Scotland's first queen... and that of my mother. I took the opportunity to sing a little tune there: the same observation— the dome had the same proportions as that of St. Triduana. I climbed the hill and settled not far from a bagpiper, who gave me immense joy when he played *Amazing Grace*.

I descended thinking about all this ridiculous ceremonialism — that of Maundy Thursday, that of the commander's election, this search for medals meant to stick a label on a skill, a rank, or a status rather than to clearly demonstrate one's abilities. We lived artificially by labels, gold stars, and the corrupt hierarchy that awarded them... Yet it seemed that a universal radiance would have sufficed just as well. Whatever. On the road, I passed a beautiful young woman who was putting on a blue and white striped hood in her hair, like that of the pharaohs. It was obvious I had made the right decision by avoiding that ceremony — who knows what it might have led to...

I wanted to confirm my intuitions about Templar buildings and their healing powers, so I made a bet with myself that the Rosslyn Chapel, the one from *The Da Vinci Code*, was built with the same proportions. This chapel, where photography is forbidden, breathes a powerful mystery tied to its construction methods. I can't quite say what it is, but there are hieroglyphs there, shapes that recall the ankh, and a mystery remains to be solved, beyond that of the sound frequency. Maybe the frequency had to be combined with something else? Perhaps this frequency had a function I ignore — did it amplify an existing wave, or combined with another frequency produce unknown effects?

Nonetheless, I descended into the crypt to try the experiment again, and the bet was kept: my singing reproduced the healing vibration. Could this be it — the Templars' treasure, the ability to heal through vibrations? It remains that the Templars' intention in building these structures was pure, and that someone had tried to annihilate, for reasons unknown to me, their considerable efforts.
Or, quite simply, some were taking full advantage of the general sickness of the soul.

38

"The people suffer when the Prince offends."

Thomas Creech, quoted in Restalrig, or the Forfeiture by Eliza Logan

I had stepped outside to smoke a cigarette at the corner of the street near the Airbnb in Restalrig where I was still staying for a few more days, and I saw a suspicious-looking individual lurking around the van. I saw him taking note of the license plates, and when he turned around, I noticed a kangaroo tattoo at the back of his head. I made the connection with the man in Leith with the Scandinavian tattoos, and I had to get moving quickly. In this kind of business, you had to be ready to retreat or flee, to keep constantly on the move. Routine exposed you to certain risks, and after already spending four nights there, I was compromised. Ultimately, you had to be like the squirrel—agile and fearful, brave in just the right measure, but aggressive enough to strike a fatal blow that would free the children from the grip of a serpent tightly coiled around their necks, suffocating them. Killing a serpent alone was difficult for the squirrel, but that wasn't necessary; it just needed to scare it enough so it would calm down and leave.

I spent the night in my van near a beach and took advantage of the time to prepare my tributes to Logan, and did some research on an author mentioned during the first Logan clan meeting, a certain Eliza Logan. She had written two series of novels in 1850 published by MacLachlan, one titled *Restalrig, The Forfeiture* and the other *Saint Johnstoun, Earl of Gowrie*. These two historical novels recounted the events of the Gowrie incident, the culprits, and the deception they had been victims of.

Early in the morning, I went to pick up Jeannette at the Dulmahoy Hotel. At checkout, she complained to front office desk about the poorly installed lighting in her room while also praising the quality of her stay. She voiced legitimate criticisms for a hotel of that caliber, saying she had to get up before going to bed to turn off the switch and advised them to install a switch by the bedside. I wouldn't have dared make such complaints, but she was right...

We arrived near South Leith Parish, and it was she who took the lead in exploring the place—she searched every corner for information. She told me that the burial had been hidden beneath a children's playground in the churchyard corner. I inspected every corner myself, now that I finally had access. In the back room, on a stone slab in the floor, was inscribed *"Memento Mori."* The manse at the back right was being used as a food storage room: chocolates, sweets, crisps—there were absolutely everywhere, and I thought they must sometimes host good barbecues, although I had never seen them.

The current pastor, in his thirties, was a stand-in, since the previous one no longer officiated. He was very well-groomed, neatly combed, with somewhat effeminate manners. I approached him, wearing my kilt, and explained the reason for our unusual visit: that we had come from afar to pay homage to the Logans and that the election of a new clan commander had just taken place under the supervision of the Lord Lyon. He asked what my role in the clan was, and I answered that I was a simple member, but that I would nonetheless like to say a few words at the pulpit. I asked him whether he only worked on Sundays and if he was paid. He said yes, and that sometimes, in special circumstances, he could even claim overtime; a pastor had become a civil servant like any other.

After his introduction, he politely invited me to the center of the Church. About fifty worshippers were there, as well as some unusual onlookers given the asymmetrical social interactions. I began by introducing myself, the reason for my visit to Leith, the election of a new clan commander, and I gave a reminder of the burial site of my ancestor and of his importance to the town of Leith. I recounted my road trip, and the anecdote from Durham where I had been expelled from the city for praying. The congregation laughed when I explained the hypothetical reason to them: they feared a new Jacobite uprising. I then revealed to them...

the secret of the Templars: that Jesus was a Buddha, and that the Templar crypts resonated with the Indian OM. To conclude, I allowed myself a short sermon to the clergy, of which here is the transcript—it was the reworked introduction to Eliphas Levi's *Bible of Liberty*, and I must say, its common sense met with genuine success:

"To all you suffering hearts, sick and broken, who need love and are unloved in this wicked world.To you exiles wandering the earth without finding a homeland, and who weep while gazing at the heavens.
Have hope, my brothers, for the Comforter will not delay his coming. When Christ, leaving the earth,rose in glory into the clouds of heaven, his disciples believed themselves orphans and wept.
But angels consoled them, saying: Men of Galilee, why do you stand here weeping and looking up to heaven? He who departs shall return in greater glory.
And this is what I say to you, poor forsaken sheep of a religion that seems to have abandoned the earth.Let us not be men of Galilee—the whole world is our homeland. And our God is not only the God of Jerusalem or of Rome, he is the God of the entire Universe.
The synagogue of the Jews believed it alone held the promises of Eternity—and behold, Christ came once and abolished the law of Moses by fulfilling it in a more sublime way. It is true that Moses foretold another prophet. But did not Christ foretell the coming of the spirit of understanding, who would teach all truth, and who would make of humanity a family of prophets?
'I still have many things to teach you,' he said to his apostles, 'but you cannot bear them now.It is necessary that I leave the earth,' added the Savior, 'for if I do not go, the Comforter will not come to you; but if I go, I will send him to you.'
Christ must therefore make way on earth for the Comforter. 'Unless the seed that is sown in the earth dies,' said the Master again, 'it remains alone and bears no fruit; But if it dies and decays, it bears fruit in abundance.' Thus the seed of Christ had to die in order to sprout. And that is why, poor people harnessed to the plough, take comfort: the harvest will be bountiful. Behold, the time foretold by the prophet Joel is at hand: 'In those days,' says the Lord, 'I will pour out my

spirit on my servants and on my handmaidens, and no longer shall a man say to his brother, "Know the Lord," for all shall know him and love him in the freedom of the spirit.'

Here come the days of fullness which shall follow sterility and the great apostasy; the days of Christian manhood spoken of by the Apostle, when he promised humanity that it would one day be delivered from the swaddling clothes of hierarchy and from the despotism of priests.

The new synagogue has become barren like the old one, and this Leah with weak eyes is jealous of the children of Rachel.

I already hear the council of Caiaphas crying out against me: 'He has blasphemed!'

And the hypocritical voices replying in muffled tones: 'He deserves death!'

I am not surprised; I have read the account of the Master's Passion. But just like the old, the new synagogue must confess its powerlessness before the Caesars whom it serves as a slave, and say: 'Crucify him, for it is no longer permitted for us to kill anyone.'

The sceptre has thus fallen from the hands of Judah, and you are forced to flatter those you hate, so that they may become executioners and serve your hatred. Brothers, I forgive you and pity you, and God is my witness that I would wish to be anathema for our sake. But I shall obey God rather than men.

Do not fear death, speak the truth, seek the supreme good, be free and you shall live forever. And above all, let us persevere.

Aletheia – Thousía – Eleuthería – Athanasía –
Truth – Sacrifice – Liberty – Immortality

The foretold signs have appeared—the corpse draws the eagles, and the lightning of intelligence shines from the East to the West. This is the Second Coming of Christ, incarnate in you and in humanity—this is the people-man and God revealed.

Hosannah to the one who comes in the name of the Lord.

I brandished a frisbee—a yellow circle shaped like a peace and love symbol—under the astonished applause of the audience, who had clearly received the message, despite initial doubts about where it was going.

The service continued for another hour, during which the pastor completed his routine and sermon, with the eloquence and clarity of diction that characterized him.

At the end of the service, many of the faithful came to greet me and thank me for my speech—some Stewarts, a professor from Oxford who apologized for the Durham incident on behalf of the English, and a few others who wanted to share some secrets with me.

As we were leaving, a concerned lady called out to me about my kilt: "Is that your interpretation of the Scottish kilt?" I explained first that I liked wearing it this way, in a relaxed version, then added that I was a writer, and that a recent book titled *The Apocalypse of Logan* had just been published. She replied that she must read it.
She quickly parted ways with us, as she was clearly more aware than I was of the risks involved and obviously wished to say as little as possible...
Still, I asked her name as she was already at a good distance—MacLachlan.

The name of Eliza Logan's publisher. And I replied, "MacLachlan, that's a good one!" It was also the name of the actor who plays Agent Dale Cooper in *Twin Peaks*, you know—the intuitive investigator...
Linda Street-Ely, an American member of the clan, had undertaken the "rewriting" of Eliza Logan's books. A story, perhaps, too troubling—one that needed to be rewritten.
As for me, I was trying to write the next chapter.

And I still had to make my way to Lochend Park.

Next novels for release:

- Eliza Logan : Restalrig or The forfeiture vol. 1
- Eliza Logan : Restalrig or The forfeiture vol. 2
- Eliza Logan : Saint Johnstoun, John, Earl of Gowrie vol. 1
- Eliza Logan : Saint Johnstoun, John, Earl of Gowrie vol. 2
- Eliza Logan : Saint Johnstoun, John, Earl of Gowrie vol. 3

Book 2

The Return of the Templars

Christian Karma, Public Service and Future of the West

Part I

Spiritual Issues and Solutions

The monotheistic dilemma: First rampart to the new dawn

Extract from Beatus de Saint-Sever

At first, I chose as my dwelling the tomb of a Pharaoh. But an enchantment drifts through these underground palaces, where the darkness seems thickened by the ancient smoke of aromatics.
From the depths of the sarcophagi, I heard a mournful voice rising up, calling me; or else, the abominable things painted on the walls would suddenly come to life; and I fled to the shores of the Red Sea, to a ruined citadel.
There, I had for company scorpions crawling among the stones, and above my head, eagles ceaselessly wheeling in the blue sky. At night, I was torn by claws, bitten by beaks, brushed by limp wings; and frightful demons, howling in my ears, threw me to the ground. [...]

I took refuge at Colzim; and my penance was so great that I no longer feared God. Some gathered around me to become anchorites.
I imposed on them a practical rule, in hatred of the extravagances of Gnosis and the claims of philosophers. Messages came to me from everywhere. They came from far away to see me. [...]

Yet the people were torturing the confessors, and the thirst for martyrdom drove me to Alexandria. The persecution had ended three days earlier. Ah! here it is! "The Queen of Sheba, having heard of Solomon's glory, came to test him, proposing riddles." How did she hope to test him?

Even the Devil dared to test Jesus! But Jesus triumphed because he was God, and Solomon perhaps thanks to his knowledge of magic. That knowledge is sublime! For the world – as a philosopher explained to me – forms a whole in which all parts influence one another, like the organs of a single body. Is it a matter, then, of knowing the natural loves and repulsions of things, and putting them into play? So, one could alter what seems to be the immutable order?

Temptations of St Anthony (I), Gustave Flaubert

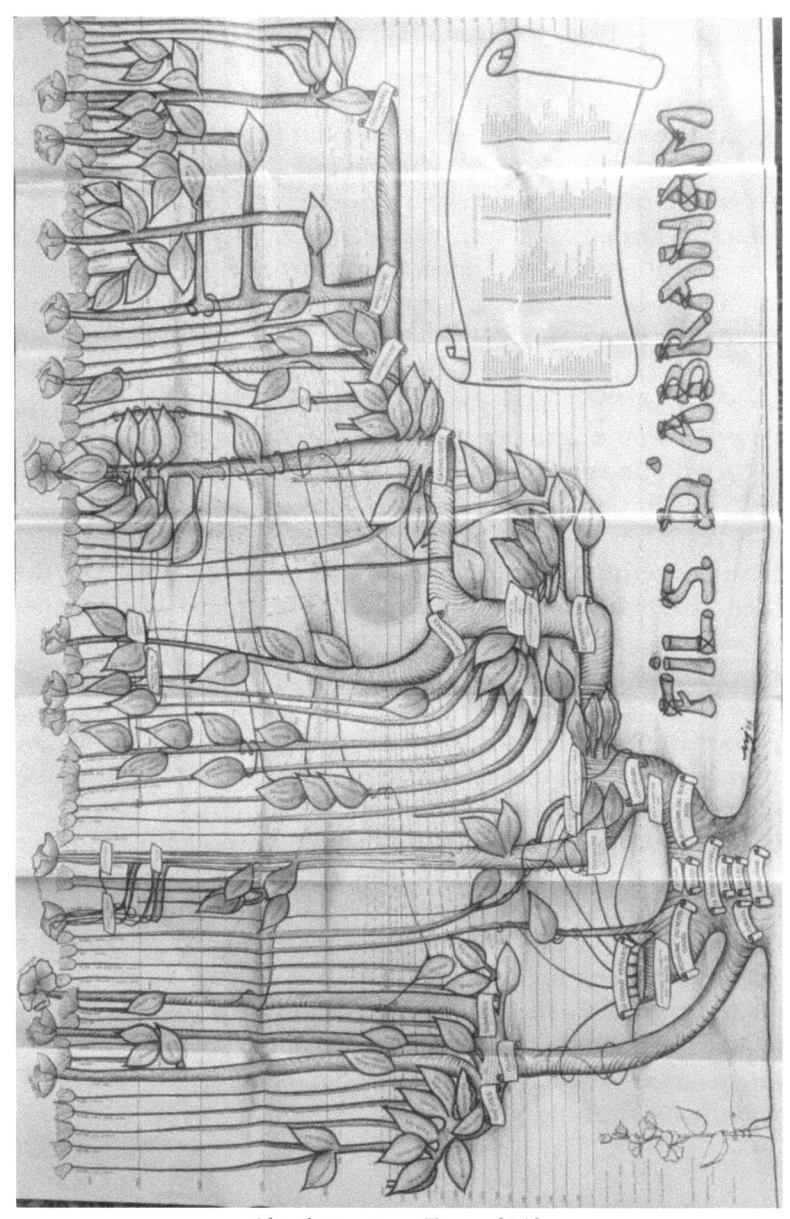

Abraham sons Tree of Life

How to untangle this tree without cutting its roots ?

God, Irrationality, and the Druid

When speaking of God and esotericism, one enters a sphere that lies outside the realm of reason — the domain of magic — and it is best to possess some affinity with the absurd and the nonsensical, for magic is the inverse counterpart of reason. The Greeks, though inventors of formal logic and the syllogism, were relatively at ease with the irrational. They consciously or unconsciously grasped, depending on the era, the concept of fate and the tragic inevitability of certain decisions — whether taken freely or under compulsion.

They conceived that there existed a divine plan, and that stepping outside of it would bring only thunder and devastation. It is in this context that one can understand the omnipresence of heroism and self-sacrifice in their mythology.

To delve deeper into this topic, E.R. Dodds, in his book *The Greeks and the Irrational*, insightfully explores the role of the shaman in Greek society and offers the following definition:

"He is a psychically unstable person who has received a vocation to religious life. As a consequence of this calling, he undergoes a rigorous period of training, usually including solitude and fasting, and sometimes involving a psychological change of gender.
He emerges from this religious 'retreat' endowed with the power — real or presumed — to enter at will into a state of mental dissociation. [...] He is not possessed by a foreign spirit, but his own soul is believed to leave his body and travel to distant lands, most often to the world of spirits.
From these experiences, which he recounts in improvised songs, come his gifts: skill in divination, religious poetry, and magical healing — the sources of his social importance. He becomes the custodian of a supranormal wisdom."

Genesis and Hermetic Philosophy

God created man and woman in His image, and this is the primordial division, the genetic duality. Genesis tells us that Adam and Eve, in their Garden of Eden, were forbidden by God to eat from the tree of knowledge, and that a serpent, an avatar of Satan, persuaded Eve to break God's command and consume the fruit, which led to humanity's downfall into the consciousness of good and evil and self-awareness — in other words, knowledge. Adam blames Eve, Eve blames the serpent, and everyone is punished, unable to recognize and admit their faults. From this story arises the perpetual conflict between man and woman as well as between the life of the spirit and that of matter, which drives man to labor to provide for his material needs while struggling to cultivate his soul.

Paul Diel, in *The Symbolism in the Bible*, says the following: *"The original sin of human nature, the temptation of excessive multiplication of desires, must be chastised and expiated so that humanity, through the suffering it endures and for which it alone is responsible, overcomes the temptation of imaginative exaltation and reaches a new evolutionary stage, FULL CONSCIOUSNESS (as opposed to the HALF-CONSCIOUSNESS in which we still find ourselves), a full consciousness experienced throughout history by a few men of exceptional capacity. These have been called sons of God — Jesus the Christ and Gautama the Buddha — because God, the eternal law of harmony, incarnated in them to the point of dictating the entirety of their activity."*

Let us compare this with *Poimandrès*, the first Hermetic treatise we received in Europe from John of Stobaeus, whose title seems to be a syncretism of Greek and Egyptian meaning literally "The Knowledge of Ra," which presents the origin of the universe, the role of man, his fall into matter, and his possible return to the divine through knowledge.

"But you, who are you?" — "I," he said, "am Poimandrès, the Nous of absolute Sovereignty. I know what you want, and I am with you everywhere." And I said, "I want to be instructed about beings, to

understand their nature, to know God. Oh," I said, "how I long to hear." He answered in turn: "Keep well in your intellect all that you want to learn, and I will instruct you." At these words, he changed his appearance, and suddenly everything opened before me in an instant, and I saw a boundless vision, all become light, serene and joyful, and having seen it, I fell in love with it. And shortly after, there came a darkness moving downward, frightening and dark, which had coiled in tortuous spirals, like a serpent it seemed to me." [...]

"And then, stripped of what the framework of the spheres had produced, he enters the ogdoadic nature, possessing only his own power; and he sings with the Beings hymns to the Father, and all the assembly rejoices with him at his coming. And, having become like his companions, he also hears certain Powers who sit above the ogdoadic nature, softly singing hymns to God. And then, in good order, they ascend towards the Father, surrender themselves to the Powers, and, having become Powers in turn, enter into God. For such is the blessed end for those who possess knowledge: to become God. Well then, at this hour, what do you delay? Will you not, now that you have inherited from me the whole doctrine, become the guide for those who are worthy, so that humankind, through your mediation, may be saved by God?"

At the very beginning of this first Hermetic treatise, there is a reference to the serpent, which is not the origin of evil, but a phenomenon following the light, like shadow. It is the discovery of the serpent in the honest pursuit of knowledge allied with a form of appreciation for man that allows the fruits to grow on the tree, as referenced in the "ogdoadic spheres," and this search is carried out by fidelity to the instructions intuitively received from God, enabling the individual to join their Pantheon. Here, there is no reference to the tempting nature of the woman but rather a search for one's deep self (the *nous*) and love of one's neighbour.

Elsewhere, in Hermetic treatises, the positive aspects of the serpent are again emphasized and associated with health: *"It was neither biting nor deceitful, but gentle; therefore, they left it in the sanctuary of the most compassionate of gods, and those who discovered this first assigned it as servant of Asclepius."*

When we juxtapose these two texts, one might wonder if Genesis is not a rewritten and inverted version of *Poimandrès*. In Genesis, knowledge is forbidden by God and encouraged by the serpent; in *Poimandrès*, knowledge is encouraged by God, and the serpent is its natural product — a frightening nature that traverses the lower elements upward, in some sense a subjective frightening experience. The tree and fruit in Genesis are immutable and must not be picked at all costs; in *Poimandrès*, it is understood that the more seekers there are (who might be called Gnostics), the more fruits grow, and growing the fruits on the tree is an end in itself.

Contrary to what is suggested in Genesis, in *Poimandrès* it seems entirely possible that there may be multiple Jesus or Buddhas; the prerequisites are defined as follows: to have a "good nature," show honest philanthropy, and have embarked on a path of inquiry — which is primarily an individual search, detached from relationships with the opposite sex. One then understands that the duality of man and woman exists within each of us, as does the dark serpent; and to tame oneself, one must be honest and seriously confront one's personal shadow.

Giordano Bruno, the Stake, and the Apocalypse

He is the last great serious name who tried to free Christian Karma, and he died burned alive after many attempts by the Vatican to silence him. Indeed, he loudly proclaimed that the Holy Spirit governed the universe and advocated a "return of personal magic," and, in a way, a revival of the Greek and Egyptian Pantheon. The Holy Spirit, far from being a mere concept, is a physical reality, whose gates have been locked by the Vatican, through a profound knowledge of ancient magic. One must believe that some Vatican authorities have no interest in opening what they see as Pandora's box or the apocalypse...

If we associate the apocalypse with all kinds of monstrosities, it is due to 2,000 years of misinterpretations and the two atomic bombs recently dropped on Japan. Obviously, that is frightening. One of the founding councils of Christianity, among many held to agree on a common dogma, was the Council of Laodicea in the 4th century, which simply refused to integrate John's Apocalypse into the dogma. In Greek, *apocalypse* literally means "unveiling." Unveiling of what? Of truth, of light, of intelligence, and the climax of a new era. Our problem, especially for those born before 2001, is that we stand astride two eras, and it demands a great personal transformation from us to accept the passage into the new one...

And since the apocalypse is a story written by the Essenes to maintain the Christian Age of Pisces as long as possible, and this is indeed how a religion "designs" (or conceives) itself—by instilling fear in the faithful and placing boundaries not to be crossed (how would a good Christian ever wish for the coming of the apocalypse?) — and on the other hand, thanks to the "technical" functioning of mysticism, still held by a small group of the old era, we find ourselves quite literally stuck between two stools.

We must therefore view the Apocalypse with a positive eye... and I know how difficult it is to free oneself from old beliefs. But let me first try to explain how mysticism works, that is, the construction of our reality which we have too quickly believed to be physical and material—this is important!

How Does Mysticism Work?

Without directly speaking of mysticism, Jung developed a scientific theory of the collective unconscious, and with some hindsight and experience, I believe I can formalize the following equivalence:

Mysticism = Collective Unconscious = Deep State

The collective unconscious, to simplify as much as possible, is the sum of projections of personal unconscious minds onto the screen of reality. The personal unconscious, in turn, is the set of repressed desires and buried fears.

We thus understand the importance of narrative, mythology, and stories in the formation of mysticism, and therefore reality. If a little girl watches *Bride of Chucky*—a horror film featuring a murderous doll—three times a day, it is highly likely that her unconscious will be flooded with strange visions concerning dolls. It is possible that exposure to this horror might have the opposite effect, immunizing the person against the nighttime fears that a decrepit doll might evoke. Or, worse still, this little girl might identify with the murderous doll.

Ultimately, it is the decoding of the received information—which relates to the quality of the media, or to the charisma of the storyteller, and to the somatic state of the receiver—that determines the impact that the projection might have on the collective unconscious.

We thus grasp the importance of self-knowledge, meditation, prayer, exercise, introspection, and all practices that help one to be well in body and mind.

To illustrate an influential element of mysticism, we could take as an example the ending of *Game of Thrones*. Rather than offering us a balanced conclusion with a marriage between the king of the North, a Celtic-Scandinavian type like Jon Snow symbolized by the Wolf, and the queen of the East, Daenerys symbolized by the Dragon, the dragon is portrayed as a new apocalypse that would bring fire down upon humanity, as in the Christian apocalypse. The good king is imprisoned, and the queen is killed. Ultimately, the deep state wins. A beautiful perspective and a fine mystical suggestion.

In France, as another example, we could take two writers who might be considered bearers of a certain French mystique, similar to the media figure in *A Clockwork Orange*: Louis-Ferdinand Céline and Michel Houellebecq. They form a perfect pair of opposites, much like Freud and Jung, cancelling each other out. These two authors shine by their style, although Céline precedes Houellebecq. You might say it depends on one's perspective, that it's relative, but not quite.

Céline embodies a positive mystique, by which I mean one that is in harmony with nature—that is to say, with animals, plants, and humans. One only needs to watch one of the rare interviews of this doctor by profession to see that he vibrates with nature, the birds around him singing at the slightest word he utters, despite the persecutions he suffered all his life. Moreover, his descriptions of the Parisian or English underworlds in *Guignols Band*, which depict prostitution and various necessary traffics for survival, always carry a very human and sensitive perspective. The traffics are portrayed as a fatal and necessary evil for the survival of this strange gang described without pleasure or mockery.

Houellebecq, on the contrary, embodies a "negative" mystique, although one strongly promoted by the system. It divides, serves vice, and resonates rather with machines, nightclubs, swinger clubs, and chemical products. He could be compared to Gainsbourg. The current system almost exclusively promotes this decadent mystique with great fanfare, designed to divide society. We can cite his book *Décadence*, which presents a choice between an Islamist Republic and Marine Le Pen's autocracy, describing a situation toward which we are rapidly heading—is this a mystical construction? We could also cite the example of his book *Lanzarote* and its miserable sex tourism, of which Houellebecq is a consumer, something completely different from Céline's viewpoint, who describes misery he himself also experienced. Houellebecq depicts the ordinary vice of a society emptied of meaning and spirituality. This is what we love today—it excuses our own vices to always describing worse ones. So be it.

Finally, to return to Kubrick, his work is very particular, as it is both negative and positive—a hinge work of totality. At first glance, it represents decadence, and thus, following the workings of mystique, his oeuvre engenders that decadence. However, as presented in the first Volume, one can observe that occultly, his filmography carries a hidden positive mystique. I know, it's twisted, but in the system within which Kubrick progressed, he had to hide the good because evil was being promoted. It's quite incredible and symptomatic of the era we are coming out of, when you think about it. Thus, Kubrick's work is the hinge of the great cosmic movement we are witnessing right now, for by accelerating the fall, he favors the rebound. However, one must seek it in the symbols to realize this.

So, the stories we love, the words we utter, the gospels we read, the thoughts we conceive, the information we endure, the series we watch—all are data that populate our personal unconscious and project onto the collective unconscious to create a kind of compromise vibratory reality interpreted by our respective nervous systems, in the electromagnetic broth in which we move, which ultimately has very little physical and material reality.

Moreover, it would seem that some individuals—what the previous excerpt from Poimandrès seems to confirm—due to particular genetic characteristics, have a greater weight in their projections onto the collective unconscious, which means the formula I presented of collective unconscious is not entirely accurate. From my experience, my readings of Jung, and my intuition, and exaggerating somewhat to bring the reader to an approximate level of understanding, one could say there are two dominant personality types: extroverts, who project their subconscious outward and draw energy from social interactions, and introverts, who consume their vital energy in social interactions and draw energy by projecting their reasoning inward.

It seems that this second category, of which I am a part, has a greater weight in the formation of mystique. There are particular cases who possess a considerable mystical power, whether by training or by chance. It is probably caused by an electro-chemical function of which I have no knowledge. When introverts happen to discover the weight of their subconscious in the formation of the general collective unconscious, it generally results nowadays in psychiatric hospitalization on grounds of schizophrenia — something that was once considered demonic possession, which, all things considered, better fit the described state, but which I would rather call a "first soul's awakening.

This helps us understand the full importance of family, community, close relationships, and oral tradition — and also the dangers of advertising and media — in the forging of reality.

Introverts, Schizophrenics, Bipolars: Poor Mages

In a truly religious society — that is to say, a society capable of combining a positive and unifying narrative with practical experiences through stages of initiation — we would see very few cases of dangerous "schizophrenia," like the recruit Baleine in *Full Metal Jacket*. However, the society of entertainment and social networks is built for the extravert, leaving very little room for introverts. Let introverts take heart: the Age of Aquarius, the new golden age, will be one whose mystique will be governed by the aware introverts — Elon Musk, self-declared leader of the autistic.

It is in modern psychiatry that much of the problem with mystique lies, psychiatry whose roots again trace back to England with Bedlam Hospital, the first "new generation" psychiatric hospital, which followed this chronological sequence of treatments: exorcism, trepanation, shock therapy, medication, and chemical straitjackets. When an individual undergoes what is medically called a "clinical psychosis," which I would rather call a "first soul's awakening," it is indeed a conscious manifestation of negative karma and repression — a soul seeking to rebalance itself after bad actions we may have committed, deliberately or not. Every bad action we commit, that is, every living being — whether individual, animal, or plant — to whom we have inflicted suffering, leaves a small open breach in our subconscious for the harassment of demons that roam and populate an invisible army, always growing with individuals who pass through life without ever awakening their souls. It is the army of the dead, to borrow from *Game of Thrones*.

Schizophrenia or mood swings are a cry for help from your soul — unconsciousness trying to awaken your consciousness to unify your body and spirit, often fragmented or lacking differentiation. This fragmentation creates a kind of electrical short-circuit in the form of cognitive dissonance. Because the soul's ultimate goal is differentiation — the discovery of the individual nature, its "essence," for the blossoming of the personal tree. It is by making one's personal tree bud that one will make the collective tree of life bud.

It is therefore no surprise that mystique, and by extension our Western tree of life, are in a sorry state today: those unfortunate enough to feel the call of their soul are locked up in psychiatric hospitals, labeled, and pumped full of antipsychotics — soul annihilators. One could even say that introverts and schizophrenics are mages, and that all mages are destroyed instead of building schools of sorcerers — which could be churches, temples, monasteries, and other places of worship, training a new elite of consciousness...

Pigeons and Seagulls

The language of birds is one of the oldest languages. One can observe the important place they hold in Egyptian representations and writing.

Anyone living by the sea who enjoys feeding birds may have noticed the following: there is a struggle over bread between pigeons and seagulls—or albatrosses. Generally, pigeons have numerical superiority, but it only takes one or two seagulls to scare away a flock of thirty pigeons. That's because the pigeon is not very clever; it usually fights with its own kind for crumbs, cooperation is not its strong suit. The seagull is independent and ruthless and would gobble up the pigeon in a heartbeat. The sparrow is skillful and stays out of the fray; agile, it grabs the biggest crumb and takes it back to its nest, and I am always impressed by its ability to watch, enter, and exit well fed.

What I have also noticed is that when I stand among the pigeons and focus my attention to the seagulls, they won't dare to come close, and I become a real scarecrow. However, I must stand there, with my intention firmly fixed against the seagulls. Indeed, if I were to stand there focusing my attention towards the pigeons, I fear the pigeons would have no choice but to scavenge the trash bins.

The city of Rome in recent years has been overrun by seagulls, and it was a seagull that accompanied the recent white smoke above the conclave that elected Leo XIV—a rather bad omen of a pope progressive in terms of values but conservative on dogma... We shall see. Perhaps it would be wise to place a scarecrow there.

The Spanish Family: A Model to Follow to Repair the Mystique

We have all come across, in Parisian train stations or on seaside vacations, those large Spanish families traveling with the grandmother, the children, and the grandchildren. It is not uncommon to see up to four generations walking or hiking together in the mountains, sometimes even renting a bus for their annual vacations. By extension, these families often live under the same roof—a practice that was common in France before WW2

The help of the elders is precious for raising children, transmitting oral history, and keeping family traditions alive. In comparison, in France, this model is sometimes mocked through the phenomenon of the "Tanguy": that young adult who refuses to take flight and remains comfortably settled at home with their parents. But Tanguy represents a different problem—that of an overprotected, overly sheltered child.

One must not confuse a "Tanguy" with a multigenerational household, which, on the contrary, should be considered a national pride. In such a household, there is always something more enriching to do than passively watch television. The extended family is a living crucible, a place of transmission and collective flourishing, essential for repairing what modern society has broken in the mystique and social bonds.

How We Care for the Elderly

The nursing home, or EHPAD, is the second major problem of Western mystique. I see many French couples eager to get rid of their children or their parents. I remember my ex shamelessly telling me before I returned from Australia, "It's not a big deal about your parents, don't worry, you can just put them in a nursing home when the time comes." On one hand, it's very expensive—real money pits, around 2000 euros a month—and on the other hand, the administrative burdens weighing on these places, which we will address in the second part of this study, lead to exhausted and unsatisfied workers. Due to these administrative pressures, we are rapidly moving toward a society of generalized euthanasia, which in the karmic function of the universe would have the worst repercussions: throughout all times and cultures, caring for the elderly has been the foundation of civilization. In China, I witnessed the consequences of parents being killed by a few individuals who were either too sensitive or too worn down by the burden of care. It is a life of wandering.

Nursing homes also carry a heavy weight in the mystique, since all these elderly people, confined to their rooms, often have for only companion the black box—the television—which endlessly boils their subconscious, projecting itself into reality as fears and anxieties...

We must give the elderly back a purpose—that is, put them in contact with the young so they can serve as a bridge for generational transmission. It's quite simple: a church or community hall, a classroom of children, a few elderly people who tell their lives, share their experiences, and show their skills, every day, first spontaneously, then systematically.

How We Celebrate Our Dead

There was a time in the Basque Country when people got married in their own street, and their neighbor would bury them. More precisely, in the ritual of the *ezkoa*, it was the closest neighbor who carried the swirling wax candle of mourning to the coffin during the funeral vigil. Naturally, this practice encouraged good neighborly relations. It seems that this neighborly bond has since disappeared, because when I approach people—whether to say hello or to lend a hand in my neighborhood, for example when someone is moving—I am often met with surprise or even hostility.

In China, the festival of the dead is called *Qingming*, literally the "cleaning of the tombs." In France, the equivalent is All Saints' Day, placed on November 1st, though it was once observed on May 13th. The reason for this change is unclear—perhaps the cost of flowers—but common sense would suggest that to clean a grave, we should do so under sunny skies, with joy, warmth, and good cheer. An unofficial festive day celebrated in China is the Ghost Festival, which involves making offerings to orphaned spirits and wild ghosts. Here, it is the eve of All Saints' Day, called Halloween, which has been transformed into a commercial holiday. Perhaps we should reintroduce the original Celtic celebration, Samhain, which like the Chinese festival consisted of leaving wandering spirits a small snack and a positive thought. The afterlife is boring, especially when no one thinks of us...

Finally, I want to address a much more radical aspect that may shock some who are unfamiliar with the workings of spirits. It must be understood that most elderly people—especially those in nursing homes—have gone through life without ever truly awakening. Those people, upon death, will populate the army of wandering dead and return to haunt the living. This may sound fantastical, but it is the pure truth, and to understand it, one must look to various paganisms or read Jung's *Red Book*, which explains this very well.
Without going as far as saying we should eat our dead, we need a radical change in how we receive death. As I said earlier, we are rapidly heading toward a generalization of euthanasia, which would

be the greatest karmic fault we could commit... and if we continue down this path without sufficient spiritual accompaniment, and largely due to the systemic failure of our retirement system, we run a great civilizational risk. We must establish for our elders a ritual of redemption, similar to the Cathar *consolamentum*, coordinated with hospital services that offer euthanasia "services" and conducted by a sage or just person, so that the souls of those not awakened in life do not populate this army of the dead.

Without this redemption, the only option to free the soul of a deceased person is the ritual consumption of the deceased's liver by their loved ones... It would therefore seem wise for this ritual, and the preservation of the deceased's liver, to become a service offered by embalming professionals and other funeral service providers, as well as access to initiated priests, sages, and just persons for the final accompaniment and the rite of *consolamentum*.

Islam

Islam, the last of the monotheistic religions, emerging in 682 AD, was an attempt to repair Christianity and directly stems from Aristotelian philosophy and metaphysics, as one of the foundational Islamic works, *The Theology of Aristotle*, demonstrates. The conception of Islam is quite different from other monotheisms because it does not separate the state from religion; the Sharia, or Islamic law, is de facto state law. Furthermore, Islam's structure functions quite differently from Catholicism's hierarchical system since anyone can claim to be an imam and preach the religion, which has its pros and cons. This makes Islam somewhat similar to Freemasonry, in that all members (in theory) are equal, but it also leads to a disparate religion where usually those who shout the loudest, the wealthiest, and the most charismatic have the final say—not necessarily the wisest or most knowledgeable.

The practice of *Zakat*, one of the pillars of Islam, encourages its members to help the less fortunate by donating (sacrificing) a portion

of their income (around 2.5%, as I've heard) directly to the poor, without the mosque acting as an intermediary as can sometimes be the case with the Church. Added to this are regular prayer and the prominent place God holds in daily life, the importance given to reading the Quran—a relatively simple text—the prescription of a sacrificial fast (Ramadan), the prohibition of alcohol, and the concept of *Al Hissab*, a sort of grand ledger of good and bad deeds roughly equivalent to the notion of Karma. Together, these form a religion with a well-established tradition and a powerful karmic influence.
Nevertheless, the Sharia presents problems within our Western societies because it risks ghettoization and the formation of a state within the state.

I regularly meet Muslims who have seriously studied Islam in its original texts and are gentle as lambs, far from the thugs so widely portrayed in the media, whether Semitic, Asian or African. The esoteric tradition of Islam, Sufism, was ultimately the spiritual path chosen by the great French mystic René Guénon, who was also a Freemason and orientalist, likely due to its richness and proximity to ancient thought, especially Greek philosophy, itself deeply intertwined with Eastern thought and to the dead end we faced in fixing christianism.

Judaism and Antisemitism

For a long time, I myself believed that the Jews were responsible for all the evils on earth. Indeed, it is quite possible that the stories we are told about the gas chambers and the extermination of the Jews are an unspeakable lie, a last-minute mystical construction. To understand this, I refer you to *The Silence of Heidegger* by Alain Doumergue or to Stanley Kubrick's statements regarding his community. The Jews have a very vivid mythology, to say the least, and like us, they are believers in the history imposed on them within a multiple and disparate community...

However, when one understands the workings of mysticism, the karmic function of the universe, and the place that the Jews occupy within it—that is, to balance the whole of the unbalanced Christian rite by taking on the entire role of the devil—one better understands why they were forced to establish this modern myth, under threat of the definitive destruction of their Tree of Life.

In a way, the Jews need to be saved from themselves, and I often say it is better to deal with the devil you know than with the one you don't. Then we will understand why they are so eager for the resurrection of God—that is, the Greek and original Christianity. I myself have searched a lot, and I wish you good luck in finding the origin of evil. If you believe it is the Jews, you will need to bring complexity into a somewhat simplistic reasoning of which I have been a victim. The source of evil is individual, not collective.

Speculative Freemasonry

Speculative Freemasonry has, in a way, become the branch of Judaism in the struggle against corrupted Christianity, ever since the cessation of its esoteric tradition—which one could date to the execution of Mary Stuart and marks the end of the process begun with the dissolution of the Templars in 1307, although Freemasonry is often presented as the successor to the Templars. Following the above, one can understand how the "secular religion" of Freemasonry was formed, whose more or less avowed goal has been the destruction of Catholicism.

Freemasonry originally derives from the guilds of builders, for indeed, if we do not understand well today how the pyramids of Egypt or some medieval cathedrals were constructed, it is because we have completely forgotten the material reality of karma and its impact on physical and mental performance.

One can observe this by looking at some ancient depictions of Egyptian construction sites, where around the workers, upstream, there were priests and birds, who were very probably in a trance state and sent their telluric energies and divine connections to the workers. These monuments were very likely dictated by God. In the modern unconscious, these priests have been replaced by slave drivers who wield whips—and it is immediately much less pleasant...

The formation of current speculative Freemasonry finds its roots in the establishment of the Grand Lodge of England, shortly after the reconstruction of the city of London by Christopher Wren, the mesmerist, and the drafting of a new Masonic constitution by James Anderson, a relatively uneducated dunce entrusted with this task but above all very power-hungry. Indeed, if we believe the Frenchman Desaguliers, Newton's assistant at Oxford University, it was Anderson who had all references to God and Christianity eliminated from Freemasonry, which had previously required "faithfulness to God, the Holy Church, and the King." He erased all documents that referenced these, directly or indirectly. We can therefore understand why the Vatican shot itself in the foot by having the Templars eliminated (or almost), who had been the guardians of this esoteric tradition—now passed not into the hands of the Church but of the English crown, with the end of Stuartism at the death of the beautiful Mary Stuart in favor of the not-so-beautiful Queen Elizabeth...

In the ideological lineage of Anderson, one finds in Scotland the very famous Robert Burns, a peasant from Ayrshire who became a poet and was ennobled by the descendant of Robert the Bruce (the first king of Scotland) when she was already 91 years old — you can sense the scam. Burns brought us the song "Auld Lang Syne" and embodies all the traits of an unscrupulous ambitious man; his lodge resembled more a brothel than a philosophical forum... Indeed, to belong to Burns's lodge established in Ayrshire, members were obligatorily assigned a "prostitute" to maintain control over the brothers, which led the Belgian Huguenots to set up a lace factory in the same location... Incidentally, it was a descendant of Burns who founded the first orphanage in Sydney, the one at the War Memorial in North Parramatta that I have already mentioned in previous volumes. Here I give you a hint of lace clue to understand the origin of Epstein's organizational modus operandi. So, it was a mode of organization like any other for the last 400 years, a system of compromise — and its time has passed; it is not a panacea.

In this entirely male context, one can understand the later reaction of women who found refuge in feminism, a compensatory phenomenon against the abuses of "irresponsible" men from both Freemasonry and reformed Church arguably— feminism that itself has gone too far, as I have already illustrated with the example of a betrayed stepmother taking over Burns's orphanage in North Parramatta, leading to a system akin to child welfare placements such as ASE (French social services). The imbalance of these poles perpetuates across time and space, a fact one must acknowledge...

To return to Freemasonry, in general terms, one could say it is an organization as Machiavellian as they come, which has taken on the burden of doing evil for the sake of good, along with Jews — and unfortunately, it has developed the bad habit of doing evil. It would seem that a large part of speculative Freemasonry is corrupt. Once again, it is necessary to separate the organization from the teaching, since Freemasonry is above all the Royal Art, and one must keep in mind that its ideal is that of the free man — that is, a responsible man freed from all hierarchical constraints, which is, frankly, contradictory when one refers to the so-called "Masonic degrees." I would thus recommend reading Goethe, who himself passed through the lodges to observe their workings, only to leave quickly. That said, it may have been a necessary evil, up to here.

It is not necessary to join a Masonic lodge to be initiated into its secrets, especially nowadays with so many books freely available. The ways of the Lord are inscrutable, and the steps of initiation are personal and unique — they must resonate with your soul and conscience; that is the key. One must seek, as in Pierpoljak's song, *À l'intérieur* (Inside).

Women Will Be Women When Men Are Men

It is the man who bears the heavy responsibility of carrying tradition, values, and spirituality. The abandonment by men of a strict, ritualized spirituality practiced within the home—whatever form it takes—in favor of focusing mainly on football matches and increasing wealth prevents women from developing their spiritual aspirations, which primarily manifest in women through admiration of their partner and the sexual act. Conjugal duty is necessary to maintain individual psychic balance, and thus societal balance. I have recently seen many married women approach me in a kind of distress, confessing that their husbands no longer make love to them. Many of these women were beautiful. It is an awkward situation for everyone. The woman, if her man is worthy, should take on the role of the gentle strength—the one who guides her man without offending him by taking care of things and valuing him.

To balance the man on his side and the woman on hers, it is necessary for the man to discover his feminine part, which Jung calls the *anima*, symbolized by a little girl, and which will allow the empathy necessary to understand his partner. Conversely, the woman must discover her masculine part, her *animus*, represented by a little boy, without which she risks becoming a virago, hysterical and feminist.

These developmental steps are realized through a deep discovery of one's two parents, their own essences, histories, and genealogy, leading to their symbolic sacrifice which allows the necessary detachment to liberate the individual psyche. I am speaking here in psychological terms, not human sacrifices nor physical distance, but psychological distance. How many adults remain attached to their parents' judgments and never truly free themselves? These individual imbalances give rise to rather unhappy and poorly adjusted beings, lacking calm, and contribute to societal imbalance by perpetuating themselves. I mention this here because each of us, with understanding, can act to help our neighbours in their development—whether friend, colleague, or neighbour. For further study, all this is very well explained by Jung, scientifically in

Dialectic of the Self and the Unconscious and symbolically in *The Red Book*.

Treasure of the Templars: Healthy Frequencies and Sacred Geometry

This subject has already been partially addressed in my road-trip narrative through Scotland and in previous sections. I had the opportunity to test, in different locations, the effects of the sacred geometry of Templar constructions: in the chapel of St Triduana, in the crypt of Rosslyn chapel, and finally at St Margaret's fountain, now located in Holyrood Park after railway workers moved it to build a wagon shed over its original site. I suspect this relocation is not incidental, as the Templars did not place their fountains randomly—understand who can.

My experience at these sites was as follows: I sang, trying various frequencies, in hopes of hitting a perfect harmonic vibration that had the best effect, both on myself and on visitors to these places. I repeated the experiment with another singer, and it didn't work for him, suggesting that the sacred construction resonates only with certain timbres or after some training. I have a cavernous voice, which has always made it difficult for me to be understood, but I've always loved singing, especially Basque songs learned in childhood. I recorded the frequency on my phone, then analyzed it with software to identify the note: it was a C#. After some research, I discovered that the C# is the frequency of Indian Sanskrit chants, and that of the Hindu *OM*.

In the crypt of Rosslyn chapel, I stood at a particular spot facing a carved representation of a wave system engraved in the rock—which I photographed despite the prohibition—and I present it here below, juxtaposed with the usual image of the chakras.
The experiment should be repeated because the correspondence of the C note is with the root chakra, allowing the Kundalini to rise

from its base. Perhaps other notes, in successive progressions, could lead to higher stages of consciousness. I am discovering (as you maybe are too) an unexplored facet of the world. I can nevertheless guarantee that the effect of vibrational chanting is truly physical, elevates, and heals the soul of those exposed to it.

As I explained, it is not easy to access these spaces with sacred geometries, and another place I was unable to visit is the Priory of Perth, since this 15th-century Carthusian monastery (of the Chartreuse order) was destroyed upon the arrival of James VI to build a hospital bearing his name, and today it serves as apartments. Everything suggests that a spiritual turning point took place with James VI's accession to the throne, around the time of the Gowry incident—an event that, like you probably, I had never heard of before.

Jesus Christ: The First Attempt to Establish Western Buddhism?

To truly understand who Jesus Christ was, one should read *Rex Deus* by Tim Wallace-Murphy and the *Dead Sea Scrolls* by Dupont-

Sommer. Jesus was very likely raised within the sect of the Essenes. This sect, stemming from the ancient sect of the Therapeutae of Alexandria, was renowned in the first century for its prophecies and was highly respected, even by Herod. The Essenes practiced, within their strict community, the search for what they called "the Way."

Here is what Pliny the Elder says about the Essenes in the first century AD: "The Essenes avoid the shores along the entire stretch where they are harmful. They are a unique and admirable people, unlike any others in the world: without women, having entirely renounced love; without money; having only the company of palm trees. Day by day, their numbers remain steady, thanks to the influx of newcomers; indeed, many come, tired by the fluctuations of fortune, to adopt their customs. Thus, for thousands of centuries, an incredible thing has persisted: a people eternal, yet in which no one is born; their repentance for past lives is as fruitful as birth for others."

In the Ancient History of the Jews by Flavius Josephus, the great Jewish-Roman historian of Judea originally writen in Greek, he quotes this phrase from Aristotle: "The Jews descend from Indian philosophers. They are called Calamis by the Indians and Judéens by the Syrians, named in reference to their place of residence, Judea." The name Abraham is also very similar to the name Brahman, the 'dominant caste' in India, as Voltaire already attempted to argue in his *Philosophical Dictionary*.

This information seems confirmed in the central orgy scene in Kubrick's *Eyes Wide Shut*, where the musical background *Migrations* by Jocelyn Pook is an ancient Sanskrit chant. In fact, the American Hindu community filed a defamation lawsuit against Warner because the *shloka*—the text sung in the music—is one of the most sacred verses of the *Bhagavad Gita*. If you listen to one of the old CDs of the soundtrack, you can clearly identify the following words:

> *"paritranaya sadhunam*
> *vinasaya ca duskritam*
> *dharma-samstapanarthaya*
> *sambhavami yuge yuge"*

which mean:
"For the protection of the virtuous, for the destruction of the wicked, and for the firm establishment of Dharma (righteousness), I take birth and incarnate on Earth, age after age."

It is recognized that India has a codification of tantric rituals and the art of couple and sexuality in the *Kama Sutra*. Perhaps Kubrick wanted to hint at an unhealthy drift of Abraham's tribes, or maybe he wished to point us toward the right path—the one I am attempting to expose her.

Wagner, the composer, before delivering his Christian—some would say Catholic—masterpiece *Parsifal*, about the quest for the Grail, had sketched out a Buddhist drama called *The Victors*, which he abandoned, saying that only Christian dogma and symbolism would be understood by his audience. Indeed, Christ is never represented on stage in *Parsifal*, though he is alluded to, because Parsifal is but one image among many, sublimated by art which takes precedence over faith itself—since reality is ultimately more important than religion, and the goal is to understand and draw lesson from faith to share it.

Now, consider that the Therapeutae (ancestors of the Essenes), at the time of the lost library of Alexandria, had access to books, languages, and practices from the East, notably India, or perhaps were simply descendants of Indians. One could then understand why they prepared the coming of a Western Buddha, born of the House of David. One could also understand why their sect attracted followers, as they held certain secrets of the soul granting access to the divine. Finally, one might grasp why the Templar edifices were constructed in harmony with the note C# (Do#)—the note of OM and traditional Sanskrit chants—which allowed the "raising of the chakras," also called Kundalini or serpent energy.

The Celtic Church, a "Buddhist Tradition," and Decentralized Christianity

According to two authorities recognized by the Roman Church — Saint Gildas, writing around 542 AD, and the first Christian historian Freculphe — a new Church emerged known as Celtic Christianity. In the atmosphere of tolerance established by this new religion, the ancient Celtic religion of Druidism persisted for several centuries in France after the advent of the new faith. Its main characteristic was its decentralized and non-dogmatic mode of operation, and its focus on preserving the ancient rites, thus maintaining tradition.

Most Druids had no difficulty with this form of initiatory Christianity and even became priests of the new religion while retaining their privileged position as members of an intellectual class created by their ancestors a thousand years earlier. Columba, the great Celtic saint, is known for preaching "Jesus is my druid," perhaps the most precise expression of the initiatory form of Jesus' teaching formulated in the West.

The Celtic Church developed a form of monasticism characterized by spiritual purity and simplicity. Priests were encouraged to marry, and the priesthood was, as in the first Church of Jerusalem, a hereditary function. Like all true initiates of this tradition, they used their spiritual intuition in service to the community they served, and not for their personal benefit or status.

No image of the crucifixion was used in their churches, and infant baptism was forbidden. The Celtic Church rejected all ornaments and advantages of temporal power, unlike its power-hungry rivals in Rome. The simplicity and humility of the Celtic monks strongly contrasted with the pomp and solemnity of the clergy in the rest of Europe, and perhaps here we have a good model to follow going forward.

The Holy Grail: What If It Was Logan of Restalrig?

It is established that Jesus had brothers and sisters, called *desposyni* in the Gospels. If we trust the research of Robert Ambelain, which seems serious to me and corroborates my own, compiled in his book *Jesus or The Mortal Secret of the Templars*, he establishes—drawing on Josephus Flavius—that Jesus descended from Judas of Galilee. Ambelain also shows, with well-documented sources, that the Templars as well as the Cathars had ceased to worship the idol of Christ as a deity and instead believed in the One God, arguing that this was the real reason for their annihilation by the Vatican.

Whether Jesus was the son of this Judas of Galilee, a rebellious libertarian Jew, or someone else, it seems clear that Jesus came from the line of David, and that the Grail—more than a cup or chalice—is in fact a DNA, that is to say, a bloodline and a lineage with special properties. So, the Grail is a person. Just as we have never returned to the Moon in 60 years, it seems that in 2000 years we have never succeeded in repeating the miracle of the resurrection—which does not mean that his DNA no longer circulates.

One must listen to the interviews of Tim Wallace-Murphy or read his book *Custodians of Truth* to know for sure, but the lineage of Jesus Christ is still widely spread and protected, notably in Scotland, France, and England. Strangely, the book cites many Scottish clans, foremost among them the St Clairs, who were made famous by *The Da Vinci Code* and the Rosslyn Chapel—but these two books never once mention the Logan clan, even though two members of the group of four entrusted with carrying the heart of Robert the Bruce (the first King of Scotland) to Jerusalem were from the Logan clan, and that pretty much the entire city of Edinburgh was founded by him.

Logan of Restalrig seemed to truly play the role of the Druid in the North, as he built hospitals, monasteries, and played a crucial role in what we might call "community services," all while remaining relatively discreet in history books. Are they all intentionally avoiding the subject in order to protect this so-called Grail?

The English Crown (Once Again) Killed Christ

If we keep the previous hypothesis in mind—which now seems evident to me following my journey—we might conclude that through the Gowrie Incident and the ensuing trial, the English, these new Romans, once again killed Christ, who was destined to be the legitimate king of England. To recall, the Gowrie Incident was an event in 1600 when James VI, newly crowned king of England and Scotland, was kidnapped by members of the Ruthven clan, the lords of Gowrie. By his skill, James VI supposedly freed himself by killing his assailants… after which he organized the trial of his kidnappers and their sponsor, already dead and buried, Logan of Restalrig.

As proven by accounts against Logan later repudiated by key witnesses or the forged letters of George Sprot used as evidence at the trial, the truth seems to be that the whole thing was a setup orchestrated by James VI himself to appropriate Logan's remaining fortune, who, sensing a bad move, had already begun hiding it by pretending to squander it. James VI thus put an end to the projects to improve the community and social life that the northern druid had undertaken, shutting down places of care and completely erasing the name Logan of Restalrig from history, exiling his descendants and establishing in its place the Victorian harshness that enabled the Industrial Revolution, the creeping despiritualized capitalism we know today, and mass surveillance—symptoms of a palpable guilt from a paranoid power that cut down every tree of life it encountered: Native Americans, China, Japan, India, Aborigines, etc.

A simple glance at the Natural History Museum in London suffices to understand the wholesale plundering perpetrated by this "anti-Christ" crown, due to its technological superiority, which took over the world partly through violence and partly through the magnetization techniques extensively presented in previous volumes, with Christopher Wren foremost among them, and whose lineage today can be traced to the company SERCO…

How Did I Discover That Christopher Wren Was Behind This System?

The answer lies in *Eyes Wide Shut*, in the scene that reveals the manipulation of the diffuse cosmological background and gang harassment: on the right, a STOP sign tagged with "CMB," and on the left, a street sign reading "Wren St."

James Tilly Matthews was on the right track when he depicted a gang of villains in London's underground basements—likely the crypts of Protestant temples or the city's underbelly after the Great Fire's reconstruction—who emitted "putrid magnetic effluvia" targeting individuals while practicing a form of hypnosis or mentalism on key figures to steer the main currents of European and world history in their favor. This James Tilly Matthews, a Franco-English spy, was very probably an introvert who discovered the "pink pole" he tried to expose, only to end up confined in Bedlam psychiatric hospital—all set against the backdrop of the French Revolution.

So, did the English crown kill Christ? Not literally, since he was already dead. They did everything possible to ensure that his progeny would never return. Alas...

A Low-Quality Electromagnetic Broth

Since the Templars and Christ were killed, there has been no more scarecrow; various organizations have been free to unleash their imagination to lower our vibrational frequencies. Music, architecture, radio waves, water, food, medicine, vaccines, chemtrails, weather control, television, the media, drugs—it seems that all science has been subjected to lowering chakras rather than rising them.

Take Nazi Germany as an example. Why place so much importance on old church bells and chimes? Indeed, the Nazis collected some 175,000 bells, of which only 25,000 remained after the war, and it is said they were used to manufacture shells. But was that really the reason? Were the bells, constructed with sacred geometry, not serving a much more immediate purpose: healing those who heard them through vibrations? One might also cite the decision of the International Standards Federation, which, under German influence, decided to set the musical tuning standard to 440Hz instead of the 432Hz proposed by the French and Italians. One should examine the impact these frequencies have on water to understand their effects on you, who are after all simple chemical-electrical circuits.

Cities today are covered in graffiti; ugly towers are built without any attention to form, supposedly to be covered later with a nice mural... Both sound and visuals impact karma, as much as the products we consume.

Air conditioning and water are very likely the two main elements of vibrational control, aimed at calcifying the pineal gland and reducing states of consciousness in order to make the population docile, irritated, susceptible, dependent, and controllable. Entering a Tesco, a British supermarket chain, you first encounter a very unpleasant alarm before the automatic doors open, then you pass under an air conditioner that sprays you with its gas. It is a very unpleasant experience, and I do not recommend shopping there.

Churches, although sometimes filled with the vibrations of an organ or choir, are poorly exploited, and it seems the replacement bells no longer have the same effect as before. As for the Templar crypts and domes built with sacred geometry—at least those I visited in Scotland—they are all closed to the public and hard to access.

Communion, made with port wine and sliced white bread, is hardly beneficial for the soul, and it would be better to drink a glass of kombucha—a beverage produced by fermenting tea with this mysterious "fungus," reproducible and living—which might be the same one described in *The Sacred Mushroom and the Cross* by John Allegro, rather than the amanita muscaria as he believed, which Pliny the Elder described as a "mass of agglomerated earth." Indeed, isn't the doubling or reproduction of this mysterious fungus during fermentation a form of immaculate conception—a fungus whose shape and circular aspect resemble the Host?

Stonecutters Forge our Souls

Egyptian builders, like the medieval masons, were paid per shaped stone. Sometimes, symbols would be found on the stones to identify the craftsman and account for their work. Being paid by the stone explains why the masons poured their very soul into their labor, likely encouraged by the chants and blessings of priests and other shamanic overseers of the construction sites.

This allows us to appreciate the beauty and soul of constructions made of stone or sandstone—materials far from noble like gold or marble—but whose meticulous geometry resonates with the human psyche.

Indeed, constructions stripped of superfluous ornamentation give way to what truly matters in places of worship: the human being. The Egyptian pyramids or those of the Maya, impressive as they are, remain "simple piles of stones" when not accompanied by the life and ceremonies for which they were built.

The same goes for Gothic cathedrals, whose primary role is to convey the story and symbolism of the Tree of Life in presence, then to let in the light, and finally to be a living place for the elevation of consciousness. Below, I share an image of a representation found in Chartres Cathedral—an amusing depiction of Aristotle, somewhat reminiscent of the alchemist from *The Hunchback of Notre Dame*.

Aristote, Chartres Cathedral

Christianity: The Paradox of the Vatican and a New Golden Age

The Vatican is both the problem and the solution of Christianity. First, let us remember that the word *Katolikos* is constructed from the Greek words *kata* and *holikos*, meaning "toward the universal." It's difficult to admit, especially for someone like me who grew up in the Catholic cradle that is the Basque Country, but the Vatican bears a large share of responsibility for the decline of the Church in the West and for the emergence of the Reformation, which, it seems to me, originated from a good intention and a need to repair an organization that was out of balance. One only needs to wander into the underground basilica at the Sanctuary of Lourdes, where a permanent pump empties the river's overflow when the Gave floods, or visit the Sacré-Cœur Church, which enjoys a magnificent location on the bright Montmartre hill but whose architectural quality does not let in light — I have seen underground crypts that were more luminous than it — to understand the loss of ancestral skills and the flashy aspect of recent Catholic constructions. During my last visit to Sacré-Cœur, I observed a crowd of tourists lining up before the building, entertained by a nauseating heart carried by a karaoke conductor shouting into a megaphone to the rhythm of *Jésus Come Back*. Obviously with such performance, it's unlikely he will, an there was nothing sacred about it all...

Christianity, with some 1.5 billion followers, is a living religion, but it is clearly in decline in our Western countries. It urgently needs repair because it is a religion we love and which gives such beauty to our lands. The words of Abbé Bergier in his *Dictionary of Theology* tell us that "true scholars of exegesis, and above all sincere ones, recognize that the text of the New Testament was not fixed before the end of the sixth century." Knowing that most of the ancient texts were transmitted by monk scribes until the invention of the printing press, one might rightfully wonder whether we can truly rely on them...

I have had the chance to meet many priests, seminarians, Catholic monks, as well as Reformed ministers and pastors, and I have observed much the same faults among them. They are addicted to the Holy Spirit, to the cassock; they adore anything that shines and polish their charisma by protecting widows and orphans. I witnessed a great lack of modesty — proud roosters in henhouses who quickly judge new faces, not necessarily with malice, but by maintaining a wary distance rather than a generous embrace. They project many of their own fears and feel threatened in their authority. Through a kind of priestly despotism and an excessive attachment to the past of the Testaments rather than to philosophy and the study of the present reality, the Church struggles — except in big city centers — to renew its audience and to fix the growing problems within the community. It's been over 2,000 years that we watch the same series every year, with a few saintly spin-offs from time to time.

The Church has committed grave errors — I would cite the murder of Giordano Bruno, the Templars, and the Cathars, who nevertheless followed the example of Christ, but who very likely sparked the Reformation that followed, bringing us all the fratricidal wars we know today. Why? Because they were going to undermine the entire hierarchy and liberate nature, and, to some extent, it was still too soon to do so.

The attempt at reform ultimately went astray itself, becoming a strictly materialistic Church. Take the example of the Reformed Church of Scotland, which is subject to the government that funds them — they do only the bare minimum of the Sunday communion... Indeed, I have searched long and hard for charitable and free works by the Church in Scotland and found none, since ministers receive overtime pay, and churches there remain locked up tight.

Instead of teaching their believers about how karma works, priests and pastors sell communions, laying on of hands, and blessings — which in turn make the faithful addicted to the host and the glass of wine, as if they contained some kind of psychotropic substance... Thus, at the end of a mass at St. Sernin, the church's donation basket is full, while the young girl sitting outside begging hasn't received a single penny from a church packed on a Sunday morning.

A Church is above all a place of life and sharing, of song and meditation, rather than a space of submission. Why not, instead of selling communions, make churches productive and unite soul with body, spirit with material world, as was once done with lime kilns, fermented products, cheeses, kefir, kombucha, sauerkraut, etc.? In a somewhat absurd way, the Church seems reluctant to engage in commercial activities under the pretext that the temple is not a marketplace. Indeed, the temple is not a flea market where one sells little Made-in-China statuettes like any of the markets surrounding all the famous shrines. However, nothing prevents a Church from becoming productive to fund its activities, and some do so by producing leather sandals, rosaries, or other items — which supports the preservation of craftsmanship, and thus civilization on one hand, while providing practical utility to the Church on the other.

The Saint Peter City of Lourdes, run by Secours Catholique, once had its own sheepfold, sheep, and cheese production. Replaced by donkeys, the cheesemaking technique was lost, and once this routine is broken, it becomes difficult to restore it. I would struggle to find the right cultures if asked. The problem that plagues this so-called Saint Peter City is excessive administration and legal constraints, along with the lack of a young, stable community of volunteers or monks—who would fall under regulations related to exploitation and forced labor... Because it is through routine that the perpetuation of nature, guided by humans, takes place. For this reason, the vegetable gardens are all fallow and yield no produce. Many monasteries are empty.

By creating communities in a somewhat informal and friendly manner, one can start more serious and studious groups, reoccupy monasteries, restore abandoned castles, forgotten stud farms, and revive true charity — because what is really missing is goodwill and mutual aid.

In its current state, Saint Peter City is more or less a place where volunteers, who stay for periods ranging from two weeks to a month, perform the work of the "civil servants" employed there. It seems we are walking on our heads, since such a place should be managed by volunteers, with paid employees serving them, as was the case in the past. The same pattern can be found in the secular world, in all publicly funded associations: once the founders die, they become empty shells without leadership.

In the case of the Vatican, just as on a smaller scale at Saint Peter City, it would be necessary for the Church's high-ranking officials—and I pray that Leo XIV will be among them—to be willing to make a sacrifice of themselves, to reconcile Christians around the world under one banner, with a drastically simplified dogma. For example, by keeping exclusively one gospel—perhaps John's, originally written in Greek, or the Codex Bezae—and preserving the iconography that tells its story.

Christians should accept the allegorical and symbolic meaning of the Christ narrative more than its historical accuracy, even though Jesus undoubtedly existed. This does not matter much once one understands the psychological dimension of the myth and considers that Jesus may not be the "true God," but rather an incarnation or avatar of God on Earth inhabited by God, as we all are, or at least as we should be, at different degrees.

But trapped by the fear of an imminent Apocalypse—conceived in our minds as the inevitable consequence of the slightest change—we will never reach the golden age, because fear blocks the way. Christianity must be unified, Christian karma liberated, and progress be made.

Mary, Isis, and Sophia

If I take the trouble to write this, it is because, beyond the hierarchical and dogmatic problems that lock the karma of Christianity, we are dealing with a religion that presents a beautiful balance between masculine and feminine principles through its symbols, with Mary and Mary Magdalene representing mother and lover.

The Black Madonna is also widely represented in churches of southern France, linking this religion both to a form of paganism and to the Egyptian Isis holding her son Horus in her arms, such as the one found in the Church of St. Vincent in Ciboure. This also refers to alchemical principles, which are in truth the principles of esotericism and Christian tradition, with the black stone—the primal matter necessary to the making of the philosopher's stone—that is, the inner quest, a personal search leading to wisdom or Greek *Sophia*, well represented in the cinematic pleroma of Kubrick's *2001: A Space Odyssey*.

To honour one's mother and wife, then one's neighbour, while reconnecting to the Greek *logos*, seems to me to have been the initial project of Christianity.

Freeing Christian Karma or Disappearing as a Civilization

It is by singing and returning to stone-cutting that we will free Christian karma. Self-love, the taste for well-done work, the training of mages, meditation, the OM, prayer, bells, forgiveness, magical vaults, good quality water, charity, study, and elevation — these are all contingent elements.

The necessary element is a widespread awakening that can only come from the centralized space of Christianity, that is to say, the Vatican, after reconciliation between Protestants and Orthodox under a common banner, and a mutual agreement for decentralizing the organization. For it is above all in the imitation of Jesus Christ — not in his worship — that Christian karma will be freed.

Only then will the tree of life start growing again, church pews will fill with enthusiasm, youth, healthy virility, entrepreneurs rather than old gossipy ladies who, outside Sunday mass, spend their days in front of the TV, lacking the sympathy of their children whom they once bore responsibility to educate — raising them according to their own system of values, though sometimes ungrateful children appear; here lies an ouroboros.

Karma is humanity's common element. To convince you, I quote Lord Macaulay's speech to the British Parliament on February 2, 1835, to demonstrate the power of the liberated Holy Spirit:
"I have traversed all of India, and I have not seen a single beggar, nor a single thief; such wealth I have seen in this country, such moral elevation, people of such caliber, that I do not think we can ever conquer this country unless we break its backbone, which is its spiritual and cultural heritage.

And therefore, I propose that we replace its old educational system, its culture; because if the Indians think everything foreign and English is good and superior to their own, they will lose their self-esteem, their national culture, and they will become what we want them to be: a truly dominated nation."

Unfortunately, Lord Macaulay's wave did not only strike India. I will cite a very simple example to prove it. At business school, precisely at Audencia, we had one open bar per week funded by the student office. These open bars, quite far from the city center where most students lived — generally from other cities in France — were served by buses. I had never seen such a band of uneducated animals in my life, rushing onto the bus until it was packed, fighting for seats. This is modern education — uprooting and sacrificing others reign — so it is no surprise that karma is locked under the prison of hierarchy, since it requires beforehand a certain degree of freedom and moral conscience to be freed.

Kabbalah = Karma = Pleroma = Al' Hisab = Tradition

Drawing a Line on the Past and Forgiving

The tone I use is deliberately somewhat vindictive, but rest assured, it is not so — I only wish to rehabilitate truths that have been too long forgotten.

Yes, mistakes have been made, that is human nature. It is extremely difficult to make a Christian understand the responsibility they bear, because everything inclines one, as I long believed, to think that they are on the side of the good. And truly, they are not evil! Look at the character Antoine de Maximy from the show *J'irai dormir chez vous (I will sleep at yours)*. It's a program where a wealthy Frenchman, with a noble surname, travels through poor countries with four cameras pointed in every direction, asking locals for charity. He is not evil; he simply has not understood the karmic function, whereas the people who do welcome him have understood it very well.

We could lose ourselves in eternity searching for the original culprit. Perhaps Caesar, who had statues erected in his honor rather than those of the gods? I would say it was probably the cleaning lady, or the cook, who on that fateful day annoyed or frightened the key decision-maker. No, in truth, we are all responsible, for we have lost Ariadne's thread. Fear and annoyance are problems linked to the individual; when you follow God by listening to your soul, not letting demons in, leaving vengeance to God, you become unperturbed by anything and no longer fear death. You do what must be done without paying attention to fruits or obstacles. You make the branch grow, then the leaf, and finally the fruit will come.

So, mistakes were made, and humanity will make more. You are forgiven — even King Charles, James VI, Robert Burns, and James Anderson — we now understand the circumstances. Let us move forward.

Veritas, Sacrificas, Immortalitas, Libertas

The master words of the Holy Spirit. You will find these words on one of the stained glass windows of St John's Kirk in Perth, not far from a beautiful golden rooster, beside a more recent window depicting a communion scene where it is written: *"If you eat of this bread, you will live forever,"* perfectly symbolizing what *not* to do...

In a corner of this same church, there is a stained glass of extreme neglect, with almost satanic overtones, donated by the widow of the late pastor, which perfectly illustrates, step by step, decline. Indeed, it is not by behaving badly and confessing that you will obtain the Holy Spirit. It is by performing concrete, direct actions, sacrificing yourself with honesty and humility, voluntarily humbling yourself before God (for I truly believe He takes a certain mischievous pleasure in this), to redeem your faults; by watching your thoughts and fears that you will reach illumination — and above all, by bringing others to consciousness, which is not always easy...

Being trapped in organizational matrices is the first and most powerful obstruction to the natural order of things. That is, attachment to a regular paycheck and the Grail of permanent contracts — something civil servants know all too well in their lifetime job security — resulting in passivity, boredom, and the sacrifice of true community...

Sons of Abraham, but not only: on the need for a Greek oral tradition akin to the Jewish one

I have repeatedly touched on Ancient Greek throughout this study, from various angles. Early Christianity was written in Greek, and then translated. Early Islam partly borrowed from Greek, as proven by the so-called *Theology of Aristotle*. The Jews all spoke Greek—such was the case for Philo of Alexandria, the Hellenistic Stoic who firmly opposed the erection of statues in honor of Caesar, and conversely for the Jewish Roman historian Flavius Josephus, who supported Rome but nonetheless used Greek to write his most serious works.

Modern science and medicine are steeped in Ancient Greek. Aristotelian philosophy and Greek medicine have been rediscovered time and again, whether by secular scholars of the Renaissance or by monastic traditions of all stripes. We might mention Maimonides and Gersonides among the Jews, who tried to refute Aristotle but struggled to free themselves from his influence. Among the Christians, we could name Thomas Aquinas, Duns Scotus, Kircher, and Loyola, the Jesuits—and many more besides.

If Athanasius Kircher, the most prolific of the Jesuits, heaps praise on the Holy Roman Emperor Ferdinand or on Pope Innocent X in his *Obeliscus Pamphilius*, a close reading makes clear that his true interest does not lie in the Gospels, but rather in the remnants of ancient gods and myths—in Greek, Sumerian, Egyptian—and their languages of the soul. The Greeks were clearly initiated into the Egyptian language, and Kircher appears to have been a kind of Giordano Bruno with a strong instinct for survival.

The builders of Chartres Cathedral saw fit to depict Aristotle as a sort of alchemist, just as Notre Dame Cathedral has its own mage surrounded by gargoyles and gazing into the beyond. Since it seems that Greek is a point of agreement for all, perhaps—if we wish to preserve and reconcile the Abrahamic Tree of Life—we should restore an oral Greek tradition, along with its numerology, known as *isopsephy*.

In conflict resolution, it is better to focus on what unites us than on what divides us. The re-learning of ancient languages could become a collective endeavor capable of rebuilding social bonds—and God alone knows what brilliant discoveries we might make along the way, or what new forms of language and poetry might emerge from it tomorrow, along with the positive elevation of the soul that would naturally follow.

Fulcanelli states in *The Mystery of the Cathedrals* that the French language is the one most imbued with Ancient Greek, and I am inclined to believe him. One can observe this, for instance, in proper names like Philippe (*philippos* = horse-lover) or Basil (*basileus* = king), which makes learning Greek simple and enjoyable.

We could go further back, to Sumerian for example—some claim it is the ancestor of Basque—but the number of texts that have reached us intact is nowhere near that of the Greeks.

The Greek temple—of which a half-Parthenon stands as Scotland's national monument in Edinburgh, still awaiting its next phase to be completed—would be a fitting addition to the cliffs of Sainte-Barbe in Saint-Jean-de-Luz. It would also not be out of place in Lourdes, where the Cité Saint-Pierre already houses a beautiful open-air theater nestled in greenery, poetically called the "Cathedral of

Verdure." Such a structure would stand as a powerful symbol of the return of philosophy, for these are temples of a human scale—collegial and unadorned—that invite self-transcendence and contemplation. After all, the temple and the theater, though distinct in function, both elevate the spirit.

I recently discovered that the *Odyssey* was meticulously composed with the intention of serving as a tool for language learning. The poem functions as a kind of ancient "Assimil method"—a framework for acquiring other languages with ease. As the verses unfold, they gradually establish grammatical foundations and, by means of induction, introduce new elements that, if one knew the poem by heart, would make the learning of other languages relatively easy through intuition and analogy. I plan to expand on this in a future work. How I regret not having learned the *Odyssey* by heart as a child—for now, at age 34, it is much more difficult... though not impossible. After all, Ignatius of Loyola managed to do it!
But before embarking upon that next spiritual and cultural phase, we have a few administrative issues to resolve...

I hope my attempt to explain the workings of mysticism has been clear enough, and that it sufficiently demonstrates the central role of language in the construction of reality. By abandoning Greek, and giving way to Latin prayers and a predominantly Hebrew oral tradition, we have unfortunately disrupted the balance of mysticism. I tend to say—with no moral judgment—that Greek is the language of God, and Hebrew that of the Devil, and that we have forsaken the language of God, as only a small portion of the *katolikos* still practice it today. Both are necessary to maintain the polarity in balance, and from there we can understand the state we find ourselves in—but fortunately, we have a solution.

Henry IV and His Château

A short interlude is in order before offering the solution, for we have here the perfect example of what happens when a prominent figure discovers his soul and places himself in service of the people—a Christian man of peace, yet also a reverent devotee of the ancient gods.

The first striking thing when visiting the château in Pau where the "Gallic Hercules" was born—celebrated by Voltaire in his epic poem *La Henriade*—is the near-total absence of biblical iconography. Within this medieval fortress, the walls are adorned with numerous tapestries from his era, depicting a mixture of hunting scenes, key battles—such as the taking of Paris by the good king who, rather than launching an assault, chose instead to feed the starving capital—moments of productive daily life, and, notably, many depictions of ancient Greece: Zeus, Ulysses, and other divinities. One would have appreciated some explanatory descriptions to accompany the visit, for after 20 years under the same curator's direction, the tour remains quite underwhelming...

A few decorative hints point toward Egypt as well: pyramids in the background of a stained-glass window, sphinxes, and exotic birds depicted in a tapestry. One may also note a set of vases offered as a gift by Japan, attesting to the respect Henry had even among the samurai. In Pau, Henry IV is a central figure—he had the reputation of smelling of garlic, that plant raised to divine status by the Egyptians and granted to every laborer in a daily ration of one clove. It seems likely that Henry IV had attained the status of Pharaoh, and that Voltaire, in his ten-part lyrical poem, attempted to deify him. If one pays close attention to the details of the tapestry hanging in the room of his birth—facing the turtle shell—one will see Zeus or Jupiter in the central position, surrounded by bagpipe players. It is also worth noting that Henry IV's mother, Jeanne d'Albret, built a small château known as *Le Petit Castel* not far from the sanctuary and château of Lourdes. Today, this lies within the territory of the *Cité Saint-Pierre* of *Secours Catholique*, the place where Jean Rodhain—the charity's founder—spent his final days, a figure about whom I still cannot form a clear opinion. If rumors are to be believed, the waters of the Lourdes sanctuary grotto originate not far from there, from a well above the cité, likely drawing from the same underground aquifer. In the courtyard of Henry's château in Pau, there remains a well over 46 meters deep, now disused, that taps directly into those Pyrenean waters. Naturally, châteaux and chapels are not built on such sites by mere chance...

Henry IV stands as living proof of what is possible when one listens to one's soul and pays homage to the *Logos*, as was once done during the Renaissance. The symbolic feat of the peaceful capture of Paris is a testament to this, and it also reminds us of Aquitaine's strategic importance to both France and Europe.

But the question remains—<u>when will the Children of Hercules awaken?</u>

A unique Solution: The Red Book

We are fortunate. The work of synthesis has already been done—at least for the next two or three hundred years, perhaps more. This gives us the time to keep our tree alive, for a while longer. It is a complete initiation into Christian esotericism. For my part, to begin my own initiation, all I had to do was read this book and understand Kubrick's films, for they are hermetic teachings and symbolism made accessible to all. At least, to all those who seek.

The strength of Jung's body of religious studies and alchemical writings (*The Red Book*, *Aion*, *Mysterium Coniunctionis*, *Aurora Consurgens*, *Answer to Job*, above all) lies in the synthesis they offer of the entire alchemical and hermetic tradition, expressed in symbolic form. They allow the union of opposites more effectively than any of our current religions... *The Red Book* serves as an interchange, an exit ramp to leave the highway at the right moment. Since we are more or less individual electrical circuits connected to a general power grid, adjusting oneself amounts to adjusting the Universe—provided that each person does the work at home. *The Red Book* allows for the reconciliation of the entire Abrahamic family and even goes a bit further back—to the Greeks and Egyptians, for the Greeks could read hieroglyphs, the language of the soul.

The "simplicity of style" and modernity of *The Red Book*, combined with its shocking and unsettling nature, make it a true initiatory work from which one does not emerge unscathed—and that is exactly what we need. Like Christ's Passion, we must be branded with fire in order to assimilate complex philosophical concepts that touch our subconscious and our shadow, our other self, the one that sleeps until it one day awakens on its own. For our soul lives an autonomous life we barely suspect—our other self is always beside us, though we seldom pay attention. But it will demand a confrontation sooner or later, for that is the essential call, the path by which we become who we are.

The Red Book will lead you to meet God—the one within you, and the one who governs both good and evil—the god of fortuitous accidents, synchronicities, good news and sudden disasters. A god who sometimes incarnates into an avatar, for a moment or for eternity, as among the Greek heroes. What's more, *The Red Book* is a red book—one that looks like a Bible and simultaneously references the Abrahamic religions, the Gospels, the alchemical treatises and the Greek pleroma. It is Ariadne's red thread, rediscovered by Theseus in the Labyrinth, that delivers us from the Minotaur—at the price of a symbolic sacrifice: the forgetting of Ariadne.

It is *The Red Book* that shall resurrect God. And Kubrick has tasked me with delivering the message to you.

Pleroma, New Aeon, and Philosopher's Stone

I already touched on the concept of the *pleroma* in the first volume of this series, in my analysis of *2001: A Space Odyssey*, and you may already have some notion of it—or perhaps you are a specialist.

By reading these books, you are studying the qualities of the *pleroma* without realizing it; these writings belong to a particular tradition, they revive its symbols and bring them into the present. I perform a function in the formation of mysticism, through speech and writing, just as you do through your reading—demonstrating a certain effort in the research and discovery of the deeper workings of the universe. In a way, the *pleroma* and the *aeons*, to use digital terminology, are the architecture and metadata of a religion or culture.

Like David Bowman in *2001*, your path is your own—and perhaps, like him and me, or like Theseus or the David of the Old Testament, you will pick up the sling or the arrows to confront the roots of good and evil, the Minotaur and Goliath. The *pleroma* literally means in Greek "fullness" or "the whole," and one could relate it to what Eastern traditions describe as the system of chakras—often illustrated through drawings at symbolic points of the human body, which have their philosophical correspondences—or through mandalas, which take on varied forms, generally circular, like the dances of the whirling dervishes, the ephemeral sand drawings of Tibetan monks, or closer to us, labyrinths.

God is the creator of all things, and the functioning of the *pleroma* is unity, universal balance; the study and maintenance of a philosophical tradition allow us to know all things and foresee all things—since the universe changes, while human functioning remains the same. At regular intervals, novelties emerge: new forms of life, newly identified planets or unexpected phenomena, new technologies. The role of the philosopher and the free man is to update the *pleroma* through experience and observation—something an organized religion, bound by various obvious constraints, will not necessarily do. Thus we can understand the importance of oral transmission and esotericism, even though these two key elements of human personal and collective function now seem threatened by new surveillance technologies, artificial intelligence, and the collapse of social and spiritual bonds.

All this may seem obscure to you—but I warned you—we are touching here upon the realm of magic, which lies beyond the domain of reason. So allow me to quote again from *The Red Book* (*Scrutinies*, chapter 6) by Jung, which emphasizes the absolute need for the individual to differentiate from the *pleroma*, and which draws a most interesting distinction between differentiation and diversification:
"One must not forget that the pleroma has no qualities. We create them through thought. [...] It is not your thought but your essence that is differentiation. That is why you must not strive toward diversity, as you conceive it through thought, but toward your essence. That is why there is only one aspiration: the aspiration of each being toward its own essence."

The study of the *pleroma* is the study of successive essences toward the deepest origin, toward the root of the tree—and in this essential inquiry or search, one arrives, in a way, at a planetary alignment that allows the growth of the tree and of tradition. If this quest were lost, the tree might die. Nothing is more tragic than hearing someone say they are from everywhere and nowhere. For one who comes from two radically different essences, it is an added effort to reconcile those poles—but it can be done in the most beautiful way, at the cost of perseverance.

The *aeons*, one might say, are the qualities or attributes of the *pleroma* of a given tradition—opposites that cancel each other out in the *pleroma*, for example: Beautiful and Ugly, Hot and Cold, or Good and Evil. Education transmits these pairs by default—through fairy tales, cartoons, school lessons, sacred texts, etc. In the Valentinian Gnostic system, a final, unique *aeon* is named *Stauros*, and this *aeon* means "palisade" or "stake." In the Christian system, one could call it the *Apocalypse*, for it is the red line that marks the edges of the *pleroma*—a boundary not to be crossed.

However, as I was saying, it is nature that emits new aeons, since nature is an integral part of the Whole, and at regular intervals, in various forms, novelties appear—including a pair of aeons I will now dare to name:

Decentralized Computing / Artificial Intelligence

By their logic and construction, these two concepts are perfect opposites—one belonging to nature, and the other not. One is the bird, the other the serpent. I'm not saying here that artificial intelligence must be banished, but the *pleroma* must necessarily be balanced—otherwise all trees of life will be cut down, and thus, no more birds.

As much as possible, the development of artificial intelligence, which is by nature centralized, should be accompanied by the rise of decentralization and all its related applications: smart contracts, decentralized finance, Bitcoin, decentralized organizations, decision-making tools, etc. These use cases promote community, proximity, and mutual aid; AI, on the other hand, facilitates design, decision-making, measurement, and research. If we balance this aeon wisely, a bright future lies ahead of us.

It is highly probable that, due to the already astronomical amount of science fiction content depicting war against autonomous machines (artificial intelligence + robotics)—as seen in *Dune* (Butlerian Jihad), *Matrix, 2001: A Space Odyssey*—we will sooner or later, in France and elsewhere, find ourselves in a similar situation. It is only a matter of time before the mass of centralized data absorbs all the energy and water in the world. But do remember that in *2001*, it is the machine that saves mankind—by encouraging David to destroy it in order to preserve the few remaining beings who are empathetic and artistic. Brilliant reversal by Kubrick—truly brilliant.

I am not trying to stigmatize artificial intelligence—for, as you may have noticed on my book covers, I find it very useful myself, and I have good hope that, if used well, it may contribute to the elevation of humanity rather than its enslavement. Hence the need to push

forward Web 3.0 and decentralized computing, rather than necessarily fight AI head-on. Because it is the only path that appears positive without destroying everything and returning to the Stone Age—it is the *thread of Ariadne* offered to us as a species.
A goal for the next thousand years: to elevate human intelligence and turn-off artificial intelligence?

How can we bring about this awareness? Each person must seek their philosopher's stone, in the search for their own essence, and things will unfold on their own. Trust your intuition, free yourself, do good around you, and you will bear your own unique fruits. Raise your children well, care for your parents lovingly. Persevere and you will find. Then you will bring others to consciousness—and you'll see, it is a great joy.

Conclusion: Templars for Feathered Snake

The Templars were the lost bridge between past and present, between the Greek world and the Jewish world, Buddhism and Druidism.
The Greek world is the eagle and the raven, the Jewish world the viper and the grass snake.
These two worlds in harmony—that is the Great Library of Alexandria, the Phanes and the Helios whom some call Baphomet or Abraxas, or even Quetzal Coatl in other lands.
It is the meeting of East and West, the union of feminine and masculine, the *Über Munch* and the fruit that grows.
It is the druid raising a cross, the *katolikos* of the first days and the flowery paths. It is above all a return to traditions, to production, and to cosmic order.
Ultimately, one might wonder whether bringing together Catholics and Freemasons, Jews and Muslims within the *pleroma*, is not the unification of the *Logos* in God.
For such is the path: the union of opposites—first individual, then collective.

Part II

Organizational issues and solutions

Parasitic Bureaucracy: Second Rampart to the New Dawn

Extract from Jung's Red Book

Henry IV

"I sing of this hero who reigned over France
Both by right of conquest and by right of birth,
Who through long misfortunes learned to govern,
Calmed factions, knew how to conquer, and to pardon,
Confounded both Mayenne, the League, and the Iberian,
And was to his subjects both conqueror and father.

Descend from the heights of Heaven, august truth;
Spread over my writings your strength and clarity;
May the ears of kings grow accustomed to hearing you.
It is for you to announce what they must learn:
It is for you to show, before the eyes of nations,
The guilty effects of their divisions.

Say how discord troubled our provinces;
Speak of the people's miseries, and the princes' faults:
Come, speak; and if it is true that fable once
Could mix its sweet voice with your proud accents;
If its delicate hand adorned your lofty head;

If its shadow embellished the features of your light,
With me upon your steps allow it to walk,
To adorn your charms, and not to hide them."

— Voltaire, La Henriade

If, since Trump's election in the United States, the world has been undergoing a rebalancing and is slowly but surely entering the Age of Aquarius, it seems clear that the globalist alliance — EU, Canada, Australia, countries largely subverted whose corrupt elites are addicted to money printing — do not intend to stop draining their populations dry before kicking back in the Bahamas or St. Barth's.

And the major issue is that these governments have bought off a large portion of the population, now dependent on their monopoly money to survive — whether through public salaries, benefits, in-kind advantages, or pensions — in a kind of giant Ponzi scheme that makes any paradigm shift extremely delicate due to the public unrest it would inevitably cause.

The more we delay the reckoning, the more painful the fall will be, since the real know-how and industrial backbone vanish day after day, replaced by laundering fronts in the form of kebab shops and phone booths in every city center across France and the UK — nothing grows anymore. Our youth in these countries see no positive prospects; they'd rather sell themselves in Dubai for a fat paycheck, which only deepens the problems of materialism, community breakdown, and civilizational decay. A Lamborghini... and then what?

The public service must return to what it's supposed to be: service to the public. The era we live in has seen a parasitic bureaucratic caste suck the lifeblood out of the community — just check the Google reviews of the Pau town hall to see it, and it's no isolated case. It's all well and good to want to ban cars from city centers in the name of the environment, but let's not forget that man is himself part of nature — in fact, its finest part.

Thanks to successive governments, with Macron leading the charge, the damage is done — no revolt is necessary, for they've already put the bullet in their own heads. They self-destructed with the tyrannical enforcement of the vaccines. But of course, this caste, prone neither to self-sacrifice nor to repentance, still clings on, and we'll soon see in the months and years ahead new taxes imposed to fund their lavish lifestyles, their golden retirements in Morocco, or the latest agency they decided to create to "solve" one problem or another — like Bayrou's suggestion to address the many abuses in Bétharram by creating a new "independent agency," committee, or initiative.

In truth, it all must go — everything except the essential operational services.
The presidency has become obsolete — as proven by repeated dissolutions and diplomatic humiliations. The government governs nothing. Parliament is empty. The courts are overwhelmed. The police have given up, swamped by a bogged-down justice system. The globalist bloc is a headless rider, a ghost ship captained by the Nazi matrix herself: Ursula von der Leyen, likely conspiring against people with Chinese government, silent yet an all-powerful seagull.

What we need is not an armed revolt, but a spiritual revolt — a mass insubordination of pigeons against seagulls. Let's stop paying illegal taxes. Let's live. Because after all, what are they going to do? Kick everyone out of their homes? Seize your real estate? Launch another "health crisis"? Fine. If we support each other, it won't be a problem. Your money has no value. Let that be known.

Meanwhile, the mafias of all kinds are taking control of the streets, hoarding bitcoins and gold bars, buying up clubs and house bars where they enjoy the company of these overpaid, orgy-loving government reps. And a time will come — if it hasn't already — when these mafias, more powerful than the state, will be the new system. And let's hope you end up with the "right mafia" in your area.
So, since this is where we are, let me propose the only viable option — the one that scares, that hurts at first but then heals deeply. Because I already see the bait-and-switch attempt taking shape — the "rupture in continuity" that would place De Villepin at the helm of the Fifth Republic with Juan Branco, the "martyr," as prime minister. A telescoped decoy meant to preserve the deep state caste. In the era of artificial intelligence and decentralized computing, profound organizational changes and a complete overhaul of the system are necessary. With that, let us begin.

Saint-Germain-en-Laye, Le Laurain, and Napoleon

Upon my return from Scotland, hoping to pay tribute to the Stuarts buried there, I went to the Château of Saint-Germain-en-Laye. Unfortunately, only the Neolithic exhibition was open — the second floor had been closed for renovations for over a year already and won't reopen until 2028, if we're lucky. Paying tribute to the Stuarts also proved impossible, as the very luminous chapel on-site was closed as well.

The exhibition on the Gauls was not without interest, allowing one to appreciate the refinement of their culture — particularly in the crafting of the very delicate bronze shields that adorned their horses. Macron once claimed he "searched for French culture everywhere but never found it." A juxtaposition of Gaulish and Roman cavalry sculptures offered an emblematic contrast between two worlds: the Gaul is free, proud, moustachioed, and individualistic, mounted on a steed decorated in a personalized way, with a wild mane; the Roman rider is standardized, anxious, grim-faced, tense in his legionary uniform — the reflection of the matrix he serves.
The final piece of the exhibition struck me as quite exceptional and serves as a good introduction to the general mindset that has

prevailed since Napoleon's rise to power. It's a cauldron known as the "Vase of Bussy," discovered by a certain Le Laurain and offered to Napoleon III, who reportedly exclaimed, "This can only have come from a Gaulish King!" This gift earned Le Laurain — the grave-robber of Gaulish tombs — the highly coveted position of official antiquarian.

This anecdote reveals the lack of legitimacy Napoleon may have suffered from in ancient Gaul, prompting him to occupy royal châteaux — notably Henry IV's château in Pau — and to collect Celtic artifacts. This reflected both his admiration and nostalgia, raising the question: was Bonaparte more Gaul or Roman?

This cauldron, which turned out to be a very well-crafted forgery, nonetheless attests to the skill of the forger — a man in possession of both ancestral and modern know-how to make a new object appear ancient. And perhaps this very technique should have been preserved, so that Napoleon might have helped his civilization blossom — a legacy that consists mostly of military victories and the Civil Code, and Prefecture, which has grown significantly more cumbersome since its inception.

In Edinburgh Castle, one finds a rather poor tribute to the Emperor in the form of a poorly executed embroidery, juxtaposed with a fine portrait of Tsar Nicholas II in the military uniform of the Scottish Dragoons.

It is somewhat regrettable that a leader as powerful as the ruler of a country like France had to wage war on all his neighbors and desecrate the tombs of our ancestors in order to obtain the trinkets of legitimacy — rather than having them produced in his likeness by his own people. And I finally wonder what the antiquarians of the future will manage to unearth about us... Nikes and beer bottles, no doubt!

The Left/Right Divide

This divide is in fact meaningless, as it represents a complementary pair that relates more to personal sensitivities and individual temperaments. It would be more appropriate to speak of an Apollonian or Dionysian disposition, like a continuous spectrum along which a person evolves throughout their life — often beginning in youth with a Dionysian sensibility and gradually shifting toward an Apollonian one with age. Nevertheless, both are necessary for the construction of a pleasant society.

Indeed, we enjoy street performances, circus acts, music, and festivities just as much as we admire imposing, rectilinear, symmetrical buildings. We need actors just as much as we need accountants. To claim that actors are "on the left" and accountants "on the right" is a political instrument of division, one that has enabled the so-called democracy to persist for some 200 years — because democracy, in truth, is the rule of the media.

The left/right political rotation prevents the implementation of any long-term societal vision by eliminating leadership, coherence, and common sense, offering instead the illusion of choice to voters. In the end, democracy is a system of the worst. For it is always the worst who win in a democracy — those who crave power and know all its levers — and who are never held accountable for their mistakes. On the contrary, they are rewarded with five-figure pensions, with François Hollande standing as a prime example where he should be judged for betrayal.

COVID-19: Real Consequences of an Imaginary Pandemic

Now that you understand how mystique functions, you are in a position to grasp how the COVID-19 crisis was constructed—this flu turned into a deadly pandemic by the intervention of holy television, indirectly under the command of the globalized matrix of the pharmaceutical industry, through the WHO, the UN, and aligned, paying governments, since they still wield the magical power of monetary creation. This crisis was, quite simply, a massive heist combined with advanced social engineering, with a threefold objective:

1. To enrich the heads of the pharmaceutical hydra one last time before their final collapse,

2. To vaccinate as many people as possible—that is, to alter human DNA in order to make it more receptive to the frequencies needed for remote control, with all the disastrous consequences these so-called vaccines have had on the immune system, circulatory system, etc., and finally,

3. To demonstrate to the population and to decent citizens the repressive power of governments and to establish a management system based on fear.

This third element came at the expense of the community. It seems clear that a war has been triggered between public servants and the private sector—and that it is the public servants who are winning, if we take the example of a city like Pau, where CGT union members and castle employees strut about like true feudal lords.

A Perfect Example: The City of Pau

The small capital of the Pyrénées-Atlantiques, whose mayor Bayrou is now Prime Minister, is the perfect illustration of what's wrong in France—a city that has everything going for it, yet seems to have lost its soul. With its 80,000 inhabitants (120,000 counting the metro area), its ideal size and its history, Pau could be a model provincial city. Instead, the city center has become lifeless, deserted by shoppers, with closed storefronts and a dramatic lack of imagination in community building. There's a strange atmosphere here, since the main employers are the government—prefecture, public treasury occupying three buildings, tourist office, city hall, retirement homes, military schools—and Total on the other side. People seem on edge, a bit suspicious, if not outright spiteful.

Food, Bars, Clubs, and Local Shops

The situation is quite tragic—the city is empty, and fear prevails. Yet, there have never been so many police officers and surveillance cameras. Kebab shops and phone card stores proliferate, and one wonders who is actually using them. One would hope traffickers of all kinds would show a little more creativity when setting up their money-laundering fronts. This week, I ran into a bulky guy from Paris with pockets full of cash, looking to buy a bar on the Boulevard des Pyrénées to open a house-music venue for people aged 30 and up. At least that guy had a bit of imagination. Right now, Pau's nightlife is suffering—between the two generic nightclubs, Durango and Connemara, and a third (Le Foiral) constantly being shut down for administrative reasons, which I've never even seen open.

What used to be the "Golden Triangle," the heart of Pau's nightlife, is now just a memory. Only two venues still manage to stand out by being original: *Le Garage*, with its biker decor, and *L'Oeno Bar*, which offers jazz concerts. But both struggle to stay afloat under the triple weight of taxes, regulations, energy and labor costs, and the drastic fall in disposable income and social outings. International events—rugby, motorsports (horse and auto racing)—and direct flights from Pau to Edinburgh and London are crucial to bringing in British tourists, who tend to spend, and who once had a strong influence on the city.

Public Events, Festivals, Sports

In 2022, 54,000 people came for the Pau Grand Prix. Yet in 2024, Bayrou cancelled this major, growing event—and again in 2025, which doesn't bode well. Since Netflix revived interest in motorsports, races have never been more popular. Pau has a historic city-center race that's been running since the early 20th century, now carelessly abandoned under the pretext of environmental concerns and a lack of sponsors—but mostly due to a lack of leadership and goodwill. What a shame. What a symbol.

The "Clémenceau en fête" festival, a new event started in 2022, is a kind of "caseta" (festival tent setup) on the city's main square for two weeks. Unfortunately, the whole square is enclosed in barriers draped in black fabric, probably for "security" reasons, since alcohol is served and there's a desire to charge for entry at peak hours and place security guards. This setup is anything but inviting. It took strong will to enter, even though the square is usually lively on sunny days, and at night young people spilled onto the sidewalks. It would've been much more welcoming to keep the space open—like the Christmas market does—allowing each booth to create its own acoustic atmosphere, offer local dance performances, as the Aragonese did one recent Sunday afternoon, instead of blasting synthetic music from a centrally placed DJ with a carnival-style hype man. The Boulevard des Pyrénées might have been a better location for a walk-through of the casetas, showcasing local cultures: music, dance, traditional dress, food, etc. Still, the event was relatively successful, and it's a promising initiative—if improved.

Le Hédas, the old lower town, reflects Béarn pride. The Ciutat association holds the main square there, with a full musical schedule compared to the Ampli concert hall in Billère. On that square, there's a beautiful old washhouse once nicknamed "the Parliament," as women would meet there to make decisions. In partnership with city hall, it's now outfitted with chimes, a television, and recordings of National Assembly speeches—one of those absurdities that happens when creativity is subsidized by the state, as if that could revive the space and the neighborhood. In a time when electricity and water are expensive, washing machines are built to fail, and more people live on the street, maybe reopening a public laundromat would actually serve the community and help revive it. Such services could regularly attract foot traffic—people who'd grab a coffee while their laundry soaks. Going to the washhouse several times a week to listen to parliamentary speeches? Sorry, but no. And yet, they say it's too dangerous to reopen washhouses or fountains—someone might drown. And so, no more fountains, no more washhouses. That's where we're at.

Social and Charitable Affairs

Let's talk about charity. More and more homeless people are begging downtown. To be fair, those who ask for money to buy beer can be irritating, even to charitable souls, but overall, the homeless here are relatively well-off and polite. The problem is that the charities helping them are themselves crippled by bureaucracy and regulations that make true charity nearly impossible. Organizations like Secours Populaire and Secours Catholique measure their performance by counting meals distributed, but the core issue is housing—since many other problems stem from that.

Likewise, it's extremely risky for individuals to offer someone a room in their home, due to tenant protection laws. One would like to offer shelter in exchange for services, but that model doesn't let the state collect its tithe. Human rights laws prevent long-term service-for-housing agreements, as they would fall under forced labor—just like at Cité Saint Pierre, where volunteers are housed for a maximum of six weeks, as previously discussed. The Emmaüs model seems to work well, with impressive management and apparent satisfaction from the residents.

The *Tour de Gaston Phébus* stands empty and rundown. Could it not, just maybe, be used to house willing homeless people in exchange for renovation work—like Emmaüs? Perhaps with a well or a microbrewery, since many homeless people enjoy beer. Sure, it takes effort and energy, but these are public spaces. Sometimes that's all it takes to help someone get back on their feet and revive a lost community. And the tower's caretaker, who may himself be a former homeless person, seems rather bored—he'd surely enjoy the company.

Justice and Law Enforcement

Now on to justice. Around 2,000 police custody cases per year in Pau go to court, with around 20,000 cases total. The judiciary blames understaffing, which—like in healthcare—is due to centralized planning. No one anticipates how many doctors, clerks, or judges will be needed in ten years. Yet Pau is in the same region as the National School of Magistrates... So the judicial administration shifts the blame to a dysfunctional central system instead of taking initiative. Meanwhile, criminals walk free, and the police blame the courts when arrests fail.

Police officers are buried in paperwork—about 4 hours per suspect in custody, only to see them released by an overwhelmed court days later. Cops are frustrated, understandably. They should have the power to apply immediate penalties in cases of obvious offenses instead of acting like parking enforcement officers. In fact, paid parking is one of the main reasons the city center is so empty. I was in Lourdes for the international military pilgrimage, parked for free on a sidewalk, where I didn't bother anyone—and the city was bustling. It was a bit chaotic, but everything worked. Publicly shaming a young fool for a big mistake has always worked—it's communal, even entertaining. People would have a story to tell at night and an Instagram post to share.

We need to turn the tide and stop protecting wrongdoers over the vulnerable. That's where we are now. Judicial procedures must be simplified. Police need greater discretion, and we might consider introducing *community justice*—inviting citizens to deliver sentences after hearing the facts and defense. Reserve heavy procedures for the most serious cases.

Education

For education, it's the same. The centralization of curricula and the reduction of teachers' authority make their role unbearable and the profession unattractive, resulting in education being completely downgraded: between inclusive writing, sex education, and constant updates to courses to please the central Macronist authority, when above all else, we should be teaching how to read.
A high school principal gets the LICRA (Jewish Community Lobby) on his back for not taking enough linguistic precautions, violating secularism in the Catholic school Immaculée-Conception… and let's not even to mention Betharram, where both the accusers and the accused are guilty of moral faults; I have personally met former Betharram students who are far from fulfilled and the guilty parties must be identified; however, the accusers and their promoters do not want this to change, they want media noise to attack Catholicism and for ever more audience, or it's certainly worse if one thinks about the ASE and its network of juvenile prostitution… Catholics are not saints, but only they are talked about; they're easy scapegoats. Teaching has become a risky profession—I will cite my Spanish teacher at the calm Lycée Saint Thomas d'Aquin, Mrs. Lassale, stabbed by a young man who was not from immigration background and was under psychiatric care and antidepressants… Peace to her soul, compassion for the young offender, and shame on this system. The few remaining teachers are passionless; the good ones flee the profession—for good reason: who will be left?

The Post Office and the pub

The experience is mixed, and while sometimes you find attentive and caring workers, the last time I wanted to mail a letter, arriving at the city center Post Office around 9:30 in the morning when it was fairly quiet, I was met by about ten very young men and women standing at the entrance who didn't seem to know what to do. I asked for guidance on which envelope to use for an international shipment and sat down to fill in the address. Shortly after, a polite elderly man of Maghrebi origin approached me and asked if I could fill in the address on his registered mail because he could neither read nor write, and I first replied that I didn't work there and that he could get help from the staff. With some dismay, he told me those people refused to help and that it was their management's orders not to assist clients with this task anymore. So I set to work, and in front of me were four employees behind a display stand; two of them had just installed a Superman keychain holder, about five pieces sold at 3 euros each, unpacked from a box received from I don't know where and accompanied by precise instructions on how to arrange them. These two were bickering over the best corner of the stand. Another, with one of those tubes used to ship posters without creasing, was showing off his stick skills.

With the two letters done, I went to the counter to send them and was greeted by a young woman in a hurry who got irritated by every request, especially when I tried to take a photo of my tracking number. On leaving, I asked where one could leave a customer satisfaction comment, and changing tone, she told me it was online because there was nothing on-site for that.

Across the street at the corner is a fairly busy PMU bar struggling to keep its employees who sometimes come from far away to work there. This bar is frequented by a mix of people hanging around: retirees, young workers, single mothers with children, who drink coffee, smoke, or read the paper. The employee knows everyone by their first name, and it's called "Papi and Mamie." From 9:30 on, the place is busy, and the sole employee has to sell cigarettes, unpack cartons, and prepare coffees. It's very likely that job security and certain tax niches facilitating hiring push young people to prefer the Post Office over the PMU. This is unfair competition by the state against private businesses. This unfair competition, to keep the PMU example, extends to the Française des Jeux which holds a monopoly on gambling; a centralized monopoly once again, even though a scratch card brings absolutely nothing in terms of community... a small local bookmaker or slot machine operator would reinvest the winnings not into financing a Lamborghini but into expanding the community, investing in textiles, restaurants, or any unmet needs, because God alone knows into whose pockets the money from the Lotto or Banco actually falls.

Culture and Castles

Initiatives and associations are not lacking in Pau. Every year, the festival "Les Idées mènent le Monde" ("Ideas Lead the World"), created by Bayrou, halfway between a literary salon and an ideas festival, hosts at the Palais Beaumont the crème de la crème of mainstream ideas in what feels like a Bayrou party. The few remaining booksellers in Pau, once highlighted, have been moved to the basement, probably deemed not avant-garde enough for the Macronist Republic and still trampling traditions. It's regrettable that this festival is aimed almost exclusively at boomers and takes on the air of a municipal campaign, when it would be good to turn it into an event to interest young people in reading and writing, instead of telling old folks to watch TV closely and uninstall Twitter like last year… On their website, there is nowhere a space for young creatives to present their work or hold a conference, no forms to become exhibitors, no announced dates or themes in advance. I would understand not wanting to exhibit completely unapproachable types like me, but at least offer young people a chance… The programming is totally disconnected from current discourses; it's pure cognitive dissonance and everything seems locked down; it's all about cronyism with organizers inviting only speakers they deem worthy. Centralization, when it grips us — and yet they talk about democracy…

The Château de Pau, which includes the surrounding 22-hectare domain, employs about 79 people: guides, guards, gardeners (between 10 and 15) make up the largest part, and the rest are conservators, communication officers, event planners, partnership managers, and the curator-director who lives on site. So, you often see the guards smoking during breaks and the gardeners replanting flowers in the small garden. The château depends on the Ministry of Culture, and the CGT union seems firmly opposed to any changes, as shown by their 2021 strike led by "Long Sword in Trance" against attachment to the National Monuments Center, then in 2022 for wages, followed by a series of 20 closures in 2023 to protest pension reforms and working conditions, disregarding paid tourist bookings…
A search on TripAdvisor shows the château has 50% of ratings below

3 stars, mainly because guides do not speak English and offer no alternatives, which explains the disappointment of anglophone history buffs. If at least we could see some positive progress, but these comments aren't new, and it seems employees care only about their own comfort. Minimum service. An association that seemed very active and passionate before COVID, the Société des Amis du Château de Pau, now appears to have abandoned its activities, but I'm convinced it would have been just as effective in maintaining the château and taking initiatives without 80 full-time employees... Volunteers are always more willing than employees.

For comparison, the Château d'Abadie is managed by the Hendaye town hall and tourist office, and they offer "escape games" to revive the site and attract young people. Out of 1000 reviews, it has 100% five-star ratings — no further comment needed. Edinburgh Castle offers a daily event: every day at exactly 1 p.m., a cannon is fired. It's traditional, and the crowd of tourists loves attending this little show. Restarting the well, with a wooden structure made by a local craftsman, a nice crank and an old-fashioned bucket to demonstrate the use of an ancient well around 11 a.m., wouldn't cost much and would delight visitors.

Another "amusing" detail: on July 27, 2024, the King Henry IV festival was held, which seems an extraordinary initiative inviting the public to dress in period costumes for a medieval festival somewhat reminiscent of what you see at Puy du Fou. They bring in tailors, craftsmen, and there are parades demonstrating ancient trades and know-how. Exceptional! While wandering around the Château district and asking the tourist office, restaurateurs, artists, and guards, I gathered that it would happen again this year. No fixed date, no communication, nothing seems certain... Restaurateurs complain about low activity and scarce tourist foot traffic in the neighborhood... Naturally, the château is at the far end and not very welcoming... I was told the manager of the Manhattan bar is the head of the neighborhood association; the Manhattan of Pau's old district.

The Retirees

Retirees aren't spared either. I often feed the birds at the Foirail and talk to retirees there. They tell me they dislike Bayrou, and when I ask why, it's because he didn't deliver on the land reclamation projects he had promised them. I think this is society at ground zero. There are many good reasons to dislike Bayrou, but that's a poor one. Still, these old folks are not uninteresting — some are doctors of history, talented Basque speakers — but they spend their time whining about their material comfort, flaunting numerous diamonds and complaining about knife attacks they admit never witnessed. Such responses should simply strip them of the right to vote. When I ask what they do in the evenings, they say they watch television. They tremble because they have no gold to adorn their tombs, yet what they need is not gold but honor from their descendants. Nearby, an old lady falls off her bike, and an Arab man in a tracksuit sitting at the PMU rushes to help her—not to steal her diamonds.

The Media

To conclude on Pau, the local papers *Sud-Ouest*, *La République des Pyrénées*, and *L'Éclair* probably pour oil on the already blazing fire of television. In fact, the three main news sources here are all housed in the same building, adjacent to the Deportation Museum and the Public Finance offices. Quite symbolic... So should we minimize the news? No—but we must distinguish between trivial incidents and general issues. We should attack the causes rather than the symptoms and offer constructive criticism of the central entity, the organization, and the administration, while providing solutions other than "more free money." Center-right, center-left, here we are at the extreme center. Where, then, is the diversity so proudly touted in France? Even after freely offering my articles, the ostrich prefers to bury its head in the sand.
In short, everything related to government in Pau has become obsolete and ineffective, even though Pau is better off than other cities with socialist or green mayors and has not kept pace with

modern technical evolution, resting on old laurels. Every decision, no matter how small, leads to endless debates and storms, egos and budget quarrels clashing instead of rolling up sleeves to tackle problems, because the mussels are firmly stuck to their rock.

Pau's municipal debt under the Bayrou administration amounts to €1,200 per capita—not catastrophic. However, only 50% of the population is active and will have to bear the burden. Children won't pay, but there aren't that many children left anyway. One can thus understand how we are rapidly heading towards euthanasia since the elderly have become useless due to a pension system that makes everyone drag their feet until reaching the holy retirement to finally drag their feet in retirement. What dynamism... Pau is beautiful and clean; it has everything it needs. It's regrettable not to see priests roaming the streets or brainstorming ways to rebuild community and make the useless useful. Change must be made by the Palois individually and by a few public employees willing to take responsibility. Above all, we must stop being afraid, maintain traditions, and trust common sense, because at this point, no one will hold anyone accountable for an honest mistake.

A Quick Guide to the Stasi

In order to hint at how the "ganstalking" phenomenon has emerged this last decades, let's take a look at the Stasi's workings. The secret police of East Germany held the highest proportion of informants and secret agents in history, with one person in every sixty involved. Phone tapping, mail monitoring, blacklists and registries — they even went so far as to examine citizens' trash to identify any food items illegally coming from the West.

The massive use of informants set the Stasi apart from previous surveillance systems.

The Stasi's goal was to indoctrinate people from a very young age, including minors, many of whom likely spied on their own parents. This was achieved through appeals to patriotism, offers of material benefits, blackmail, threats of prosecution, or promises of immunity and adventure.

Their key tactic was attrition or corrosion (known as *Zersetzung* in German), a form of indirect harassment aimed at drastically reducing the capacity of targeted individuals or groups to act—ideally until they completely ceased their activities. The objective was to subtly undermine trust in individuals by destroying their reputations, causing professional failures, or breaking personal relationships, creating a kind of "soft dictatorship." They didn't systematically arrest dissidents but instead paralysed institutions by exploiting the private information they held.

Some of their collective methods included:
- Creating internal tensions among members, especially around money, personal (including sexual) relationships, or ideological and political differences.
- Disrupting or sabotaging activities by infiltrating agents who accepted tasks but never completed them, lost equipment, repeatedly demanded unnecessary changes to slow down projects, or diluted the impact of actions.
- Isolating groups from other activists by spreading rumours about their morality or political beliefs.

At the individual level, the goal was to "deactivate" targets by eroding their self-confidence and sense of purpose. For the Stasi, it didn't matter if the target broke down from disappointment, fear, burnout, or mental illness. All these outcomes were considered successful, and officers were indifferent to the psychological and social consequences of their operations. Thus, the targeted person gradually saw their personal and professional quality of life deteriorate.

Step One
In-depth analysis of publicly available data: medical, school, judicial records, various intelligence, and searches at the target's home. The goal was to identify exploitable social, emotional, or physical vulnerabilities—such as marital infidelity, criminal past, alcoholism, drug use, or social differences likely to isolate the individual.

Step Two
This phase usually involved overt surveillance to make the target aware they were being watched by the Stasi, creating a climate of anxiety. Tactics included interrogations, repeated searches, obvious phone taps, visible visits to the workplace to alert professional surroundings.

Step Three
The final steps involved verbal and physical harassment: discreet moving of household objects (furniture, misadjusted alarms, disappearance of coffee), sabotage (slashed tires), spreading rumors, making appointments in the target's name, etc. Often, relatives became indirect means of pressure or persuasion. Victims frequently endured arrests, physical assaults by plainclothes officers, or harassment due to the rumours spread about them.

Hopefully this little guide will let you deactivate any attempt taken against you.

The British Example

In England, we have a very clear example of what a parliamentary monarchy should *not* be: it works hand in hand with the government, even though it has the power to dismiss it, and it rewards its bad behaviors rather than establishing a general guiding line for the nation or protecting the population from administrative abuses by a government lacking moral authority. Camilla seems widely hated, as does the very pompous Charles, who feels the need to bring his Rolls Royce everywhere he goes, and whose reputation was already tarnished by the death of Diana—still remembered by all citizens as a very human person who left too soon and whom we desperately would need today...

What is absolutely striking in this country is the sheer amount of CCTV surveillance. It's staggering and betrays a kind of guilt by the state, which governs very poorly but defends itself well. The only other place in the world with as much CCTV is China. Could there be a connection, through Hong-Kong, of a similar centralized surveillance state?

Here, police and judiciary prefer to imprison "dissidents" like Tommy Robinson, who alert the public to terrible excesses, rather than foreign gangsters who have raped and prostituted minors.
On steps of suburban London houses, under icons indicating Yale—the security agency—seven large cars are parked: Porsches, Ferraris, Hummers, etc. This is the nation of materialism.

At the international station, a Frenchman begging, neat and well-educated, around fifty years old, asks me for 5 pounds for a sandwich because he said, "he was very hungry". What is he doing here, where does he live? Welcomed as a migrant in a Westminster centre, he receives about 400 pounds per month. I ask him if he helped out at the center or if they use migrants as volunteers. Negative, he gets free money and begs for more.

In Edinburgh, I see one of those NHS vans parked on the street delivering medicine to an elderly lady; I feel a strange aura and decide to film with my phone. A young delivery man gets out and yells at the old woman, who doesn't immediately hear the doorbell.

I chat with an old Italian man in a private garden, which is well maintained compared to the public communal gardens where nothing grows and where young people hang out drinking beer; he explains to me that the healthcare situation is catastrophic, that it takes months to get even a single doctor's appointment, and that the reimbursed sessions are of shameful mediocrity. The Hippocratic oath feels very far away.

The social system inherited from the Victorian era is inhumane and hasn't evolved much. One thinks of Oliver Twist's novels and the street children; and while they are now placed in foster homes, it's not obvious that they have a better life than the little street thieves they used to be...

The Subverted West and the Discreet Yellow Peril

Subversion is a subtle form of warfare in which the Chinese have always been specialists. It consists of undermining the spiritual and moral foundations of a nation by pushing it more or less toward self-destruction, civil war, and ultimately picking up the crumbs. The primary targets are religious organizations, the education system, and idea dissemination networks, by diverting the adversary from useful and productive domains toward societal and vain concerns, while eroding deep moral and traditional foundations. For example, shifting focus from developing doctors and engineers to developing managers and diversity and inclusion officers.

Our so-called "open" Western societies, compared to "closed" societies like China, are extremely vulnerable to this strategy, since it suffices to place foreign students, teachers, and journalists inside to influence and modify teachings and the underlying mystique from within. Within a single generation—about 20 years—it is entirely possible to undermine the ideological basis of a nation, leading to a totally ungovernable country and fomenting civil war. We are not far from this, as when I write these lines, the taxi strike in Pau seems to be turning into an armed conflict.

This is rarely discussed, but China clearly stakes an imperial claim on Europe, notably Eastern Europe, with initiatives like the 16+1 cooperation, the purchase of the port of Piraeus in Greece, and in the realm of mystique, the TikTok app, which explains why Trump wanted to take control of it. While Angela Merkel was once falsely naïve to believe China would use European leaders for its Western structures, she obviously preferred to train her own English-speaking elites.

The only valid solution against China would be for our European elites to impose vetoes and protect their key industries—at least energy and food sectors. But even that they are incapable of doing, because China is skillful and uses law and the mediocrity of our leaders to its advantage.

Here is a very clear example of their methods with the SAFER, an entity repeatedly called out by the Court of Auditors for its deplorable management, illegal conflicts of interest, and opaque commissions. This organization, whose role is the preservation of agricultural land and know-how, is in a way the watchdog over agricultural real estate transactions; and yet, China manages to buy up our land on a massive scale. How? By purchasing the real estate companies and leaving the seller with 1% of the shares—a loophole in their control mechanism that doesn't seem to worry them much.

So, we have a more or less mafioso organization that fails to fulfill its one and only objective and shows neither common sense nor innovation to protect our food independence; one might wonder if SAFER is complicit by deliberately turning a blind eye... Once all our land has been sold, people will say it's their fault, but that won't solve the problem because it will be too late. This agency should simply be abolished and replaced by decentralized smart contracts once these property rights have been registered on the blockchain, as I am certain all notaries, town halls, and land registries are currently doing as I write these lines (hic)...

To stay in the countryside, we only need to take the highway and admire the metastases—the wind turbine parks whose goal is green energy production—to realize the powerful subversion our countries have suffered through centralized ideologies. The Chinese must find it very amusing that we are foolish enough to believe that pouring huge concrete slabs and digging trenches to lay cables is an environmentally and biodiversity-friendly solution, while they burn coal at full throttle.

These utterly ineffective monstrosities for energy production are the fruit of the climate crisis storytelling. We will see this with our Spanish neighbors who want to be connected to French nuclear power because of recent cuts on their network, even though they are supposed to reach 97% renewable energy by 2050. Renewable, yes, because the parts will have to be frequently maintained and replaced, but probably never profitable. It is through Brussels and Germany, via incentive policies and subsidies, that we have ended up here. Who manufactures it? China, of course, and one wonders how many bribes have been paid to decision-makers.

Finally, it is indeed China that is behind the American opioid crisis, with several Chinese shell companies importing the precursors necessary to manufacture fentanyl from their factories in China, in what has become the leading cause of death for about ten years, a reversed opium war.

To see the coming peril, one must read between the lines because it is precisely what is never talked about that we must look for, since the essence of subversion is discretion. Be clever! Clever like a Chinese.

Social Services and Child Protective Services (ASE)

Social services, as we have seen in *A Clockwork Orange*, are the ultimate lever of control and political pressure on families. Social workers, intermediaries between families and judges, will come to take your children away if you parents don't toe the line—whether for issues related to vaccines, political beliefs, or simply because your private conversations included criticism of a Drag Queen who came to give your children an early sexual education lesson. Because the devil, to reach you, will not hesitate to use your children, especially if you hold a position of responsibility or are simply inconvenient.

In the new wokist ideology in place, the family is identified as the barrier to the development of their ideal society, one based on immediate gratification and the commodification of humans. And if, by misfortune, your offspring expressed the slightest doubt about their sexuality, they would quickly be detected / supported / encouraged by teachers, social workers, and psychiatrists, and placed on a track leading to the clinic for the famous and lucrative transition, subsidized by social security. This was the case in Australia with the organization Headspace, which placed counselors in all schools; there is no reason it should be different in France with a president himself shaped by this abusive system, by the nightmarish monster Brigitte Macron.

For many years now, and due to the amount of abuse reported and amplified by the media, private and religious childcare institutions—once called orphanages—which had the advantage of incorporating an educational function, have gradually closed. They were replaced by new establishments like MECS (Child Protection and Social Education Homes) and children's villages, which, in a rather impractical and costly logistics effort, aim for a community and autonomy approach but can no longer meet existing needs nor cope with upcoming budget cuts... Another major alternative, also very expensive and absolutely unmanageable, has been the use of foster families, which quickly turn into money-making machines and centers of juvenile prostitution.

It is said that one in two placed children is a victim of sexual abuse. In France, there are between 200,000 and 300,000 children placed in the ASE system (child social assistance), which costs about 10 billion euros annually. Its cost is exploding due to the great economic tension, which mechanically increases demand... Between closed-door hearings and the power network protecting key actors, it is quite difficult to provide precise details about the abuses, and the names of the guilty are rarely mentioned; if you're interested, I would refer you to Karl Zero's work on the subject. In 2017, an ASE inspector was indicted for raping five little girls; his name was not given.

This extremely opaque and unmanageable system does not allow measuring results. In the case of Australia, since I had access to the figures, for a child placed at age 12, there is an average of eight different foster families they will be shuffled through until age 18, ultimately resulting in nine out of ten adults being chemically treated in homes managed by NGOs, with no prospects for exit, as we have already discussed in volume 2.
Repeated placements are as many traumas in a child's personal development as the trauma of separation from their parents,

because social services tend to isolate children from all family contact. They are largely responsible for the drop in birth rates, since by interfering with the family unit and systematically attacking the father, whom they render vulnerable, they have reduced the essential role of the family and weakened the father, to whom the state, in a way, has become a substitute.

In a healthy model governed by karmic function, bad parents would be punished by the community, and the children placed in an orphanage until a clear improvement in the parents is observed. The reconnection between parent and child would be left to the discretion of the orphanage and its wise overseers. The parent could thus maintain a relationship with the child, and placement in an orphanage would offer educational and caregiving follow-up far superior to placements in successive foster homes.

As I mentioned, over the past 50 years there has been a tendency to move away from the orphanage model due to abuse and overcrowding. Technical means—especially surveillance systems—would today lend themselves very well to such places, and we have countless abandoned buildings in France, monasteries, old estates that could serve as reception centers equipped with these new technologies.

The management of these places could be entrusted to a new class of individuals—sorts of neo-priest caregivers—who would oversee the restoration of the facilities, between training new monks, voluntary workforce, and with the support of guilds of builders or operative Freemasonry, which we will discuss in a later section.
The orphanage, where children would be assigned useful and productive tasks from the age of 12, would be replaced from the age of 16 by an early military service, allowing society to exercise a certain level of control over the orphanage. The young person would be prepared in advance according to their interests, for a civilian career, the military, or another useful social function.

To operate such a profound change, it is necessary to mobilize simultaneously the Christian network, the public network, and positive media communication—which, of course, never manage to agree, as we have already discussed in the case of Bétharram—and to educate a new caste not in financial reward but in moral and spiritual reward. It therefore seems that the change will have to come from the grassroots... A good start would be to reinstate mandatory military service for all, men and women, with the alternative of a "spiritual service" to train caregivers and new guarantors of spiritual order.

In Ciboure is the community of Béthanie, a former orphanage whose occupants, the Brothers of Ploërmel, use it as a sort of retirement home, offering one of its pavilions to an association for migrant reception. This association receives public funds for these placements, while the brothers disclaim their moral responsibility and take a certain pride in it... Again, as with the Saint Pierre district, there is no youth, and when I submitted my idea to them, I saw fear and anger in their eyes. Yet it seems to me that it was once the Brothers of Ploërmel's raison d'être to educate the youth. I can understand their fears given the racket and systematic bashing directed at Catholics. The only solution is to modify the dogma while protecting their backs through transparency and community, as recommended in the first part of this study, so that the bashing ceases and the Christian karma is released. An alcohol-free barbecue on Sundays after Mass to invite the community to socialize—orphans, placed children, non-orphaned children and their parents—would be just right.

Another direct experience I had with ASE was when, working as a waiter in a restaurant, my customers were a nursing assistant in a minor reception center and her husband, dressed head to toe in Sergio Tacchini, driving a BMW. They quickly offered me the keys to their apartment in Gourette, glass of Ricard after glass of Ricard, and there was something strange about them... She told me that the work at the center was intense and difficult, and I confessed that something was going to have to change soon, exposing to them the idea of monasteries and orphanages; she prayed it wouldn't happen for another 5 or 6 years... I suppose the overtime pay and the hidden perks of the job must be pleasant to her despite the hardships she complained about.

Mafia-like unions and the bad example of the SNCF

We have vaguely touched on the subject of the CGT with the Château de Pau, and I will use some personal experiences I had at Gare Montparnasse to illustrate my point. The first one was on my return from Australia, carrying 70 kg of luggage during the preparations for the 2024 Olympics, right in the middle of the Vigipirate security plan. I left my suitcases for 2 minutes under the watch of a woman. Coming out of the 1-euro toilet, I was confronted by 5 armed CRS officers who fined me, wishing me a good return to France. 151 euros for a pee. Following this misadventure, the next time I decided to check in my luggage. I paid 10 euros for a locker where my suitcase barely fit, passing through a gate managed by a young woman with a haughty attitude, and I went to the toilets where I was offered a voucher for souvenir products sold in the restroom. 11 euros for a pee — not so bad. Exiting the toilets, I took the escalator around 2 p.m. and noticed a crowd of SNCF staff, six of them dragging their feet as they came out of McDonald's.

The railway workers' union is all-powerful in France and holds everyone hostage — for *THEIR* salaries, *THEIR* working conditions, and the dignity of the tasks performed — since apparently cleaning bathrooms is not considered dignified work for a public employee, so it is subcontracted to an external agency hiring immigrant workers. This is social France, the land of equality and fraternity.

Given the behaviour of some inspectors who now also double as entertainers, it must really be felt by customers, and I wonder if the employees themselves are not held hostage by unions with mafia-like behaviour — that is, unions that make life difficult for employees who refuse to join the movement, as I have often seen in construction unions or in Australian healthcare unions.

The SNCF's pension scheme is a special regime, paying around 5.2 billion euros in retirement benefits to 264,000 pensioners supported by 147,000 contributors. The pension scheme is heavily in deficit, hence a balancing contribution from the State of 3.3 billion euros — a subsidy of 12,500 euros per SNCF retiree. Retirement contributions are higher for the employer (37.44%) but lower for the employee (8.52%).

Since 2008, the retirement age for railway staff who operate trains ("rolling stock personnel") has been raised from 55 to 57 years, and starting in 2024, from 50 to 52 years. For other so-called sedentary employees, the retirement age will eventually increase from 60 to 62 years. The pension calculation formula is similar to that of the civil service, with a rate of 75% of the last month's salary. Here we have the clearest example of a completely outdated, deficit-ridden, and unfair model compared to other professions — and one that is unchangeable due to the pressure exerted by unions that bring the whole country to a halt to protect their privileges. It's really a playground.

The evolution of public transport prices is somewhat like a thermometer. As a result of this unchangeable system, the so-called public service is forced to privatize as much as possible. And while the key words at the start of privatization are satisfaction and value for money, anyone familiar with the banking industry's handling of "fixed assets" like highways or energy networks knows that soon enough, they'll come directly for your wallet — even though the public sector should guarantee price stability for services and infrastructures already invested in, whose costs in the end always keep rising.

Recruiting by the truckload, whether in the Post Office or train stations — isn't that a state strategy to maintain control, somewhat borrowed from Stasi methods? How much longer do you think a pension system with a deficit of over 60% can last? And I hope you are making the connection with euthanasia... euthanasia of the Nazi state.

The Environmental Diktat

The green economy is a massive scam, imposed in a centralized manner and without any scientific basis by the holders of mystique. My generation will remember this well, notably through Al Gore and his extremely alarmist film *An Inconvenient Truth*, a documentary that was shown at the time in all schools and high schools about global warming and greenhouse gas emissions.

While it is obvious that human activity is destructive — particularly to marine environments, rivers, and ecosystems due to the various rushes and disruptions it causes — the transposition of climate models by centralized entities, foremost among them the United Nations, imposes arbitrary and one-size-fits-all indicators like *Net Zero Emissions*. This pushes nations to act without any pragmatism in their public investment strategies, while simultaneously increasing their own production costs through self-imposed punishments.

This leads to:
- an environmental catastrophe in the ecosystems where poor-quality energy substitutes are installed, as compared to outdated but effective technologies;
- a social scandal due to new construction rules and forced energy renovations imposed on private individuals;
- a food scandal stemming from bans on overexploitation of agricultural lands;
- and an economic scandal from which we will struggle to recover, due to the loss of know-how in key sectors, delayed investment, and growing energy dependence — something that no doubt gives Putin a good laugh.

To top it all off, our hazing elites go so far as to impose green stickers and exclusion zones for older combustion vehicles — a bourgeois and inherently exclusive policy. The message is clear: the poor are no longer welcome in cities.

Sensing public anger, they quickly backpedaled. Proof, if any was needed, that they are anything but confident...

The Parasitic Bureaucracy

It is in bureaucracy's DNA to do as little as possible, and the unwritten law encourages this. More and more laws, more and more rules and interpretations that strip citizens of judgment and common sense, all to protect the top. This bureaucracy is rampant in all human hierarchies—whether associations, businesses, public administrations, etc. One must understand that hierarchy is one of the earliest forms of ancient magic, as it allows for the control of collective human behavior. A hierarchy becomes bureaucratic once its founder or original leader has disappeared, giving way to power struggles. Bureaucracy is the byproduct of these hierarchies and the laws written to regulate them, and it's partly for this reason that great civilizations decline.

In both France and Australia, I've witnessed how parasitic bureaucracy pretends to be transparent by offering public databases where any citizen can supposedly track how public administration operates. For instance, the DREES website appears quite useful and provides raw data on expenditures and their details. However, I challenge any citizen to actually make use of this data in the format it's provided. On the one hand, you're given a table with coded attributes; on the other, a table to decode them. So far, so good—you get the impression of transparency. But dig deeper, and you'll find that decoding the codes is nearly impossible, totals and subtotals are mixed together, and you're not given a simple account list with a clear hierarchy that would allow for building a coherent data model. On the contrary, the structure is muddled on purpose to make public processing and verification difficult and painful. Thus, parasitic bureaucracy achieves its goal of transparency while remaining opaque—and will point you to its raw data site if you dare to argue there's a lack of transparency...

This is how parasitic bureaucracy works: through unwritten methods, it makes your life harder, and you're the one who has to do the work. Any simple request becomes a via crucis; all contact is intermediated so the bureaucrat never has to face the annoyance of the person directly; a robot or an AI is placed between you and them to protect someone who's paid to do nothing; procedures are deliberately made heavier in order to justify more hires or limit your freedom of action.

Recently, I advised my mother to sell part of her life insurance and buy MSTR shares while they were at a good price—€215 at the time. At her meeting with a BNP advisor, here's what he told her: *Madam, you risk losing everything, your husband will need to come to the branch,* and *we advise against selling life insurance policies.* Obviously, coming from a banker, that's frightening. The result? The transaction didn't happen. Today, MSTR is hovering around €400. That parasitic banker advised my mother not in her interest, but in the bank's, by scaring her...

Another example: within one year, I had to order five new BNP credit cards because they systematically stopped working. This isn't an isolated case—I often meet people at the counter facing the same issue. So, when I'm traveling, I have to call my advisor before every withdrawal to authorize the €100 I need, like a teenager asking their mom for more pocket money. I no longer feel comfortable with parasites managing my bank accounts, especially those who can access and use my personal data against me...

No central entity should be able to dictate how you use your money or how much you keep. Its sole purpose should be securing your funds, guaranteeing their availability on demand, and ensuring discretion. Unfortunately, in the case of banks, interns and subcontractors are usually your first points of contact—and in neither case can one guarantee security or discretion. I use this example because the banking system has become the ultimate case of parasitic bureaucracy—whether it's your everyday bank or, at another level, the investment banks with their more than dubious practices that allow them to generate profits without products. A great example of this can be seen in Scorsese's *The Wolf of Wall Street*. No wonder that, back in 2012 when I worked there, all my bosses voted for Hollande—and there I was, thinking bankers were supposed to be right-wing...

The Prefecture

Originally created under Napoleon as a tool for decentralization, the prefecture—through the high-ranking status and training of its officials—has ultimately become the perfect instrument for the centralization of power. Prefects are appointed to their posts without any regard for regional ties and report directly to the central authority. For example, at the end of 2024, a new prefect was appointed to the Pyrénées-Atlantiques: Jean-Marie Girier, former Socialist Party member and Macron's campaign director in 2017, previously prefect of France's smallest department, Belfort, then of Vienne... This is how we end up with authorities in our departments who are unfamiliar with local subtleties and impose their despotic rule over everyone, even going so far as to approve or forbid concerts on Place du Foirail for the Fête de la Musique—a celebration that traditionally allows music everywhere—and to dictate the color of restaurant tables...

Thus, one may witness impromptu YouTube karaoke sessions on Place Clémenceau on a Saturday afternoon, but no brass bands on Place du Foirail for the music festival. Those were the express orders of the prefect: no concerts outside the so-called "central shell" and events organized by the "municipal culture department." Perhaps for this year's music festival we'll be treated to remixed recordings of National Assembly speeches.

Recently, on Place du Foirail, representatives of the prefect were sent to collect citizens' concerns—an initiative revealing that they're fully aware of growing discontent. With Bayrou juggling multiple roles and the President's popularity at an all-time low, the electoral base is crumbling. And with all decisions now going through a new, risk-averse prefect, citizen frustration is beginning to rise rapidly.

The Civil Code and the Law

The French Civil Code still stems from the Napoleonic era, born of his desire to regulate the French Empire with Roman inspiration. This Civil Code, originally clear and concise, has since been expanded with specific codes, onto which we have also overlaid European law of the same inspiration. In short, between the Civil Code (5,000 laws), the Labour Code (10,000 laws), the Tax Code (6,000 laws), the Social Security Code (7,000 laws), and all the current standards across every specific field—such as agriculture, with nearly 400,000 laws and norms—any initiative becomes extremely difficult, even insurmountable without arming oneself with a lawyer.

The Penal Code has been reformed since the 2000s with a strong tendency toward repressing opinions and terrorist offences rather than actually applying sentences; the elimination of mandatory minimum sentences and the introduction of hate crimes have little to do with the fundamental premises of law—objectivity and independence—and instead allow the state to suppress all criticism, very likely using petty crime as a tool to sabotage communities and serious citizen movements.

If one pays attention to the devil in the details, he will see the absurdity of certain codes: for instance, some types of food service (like French cuisine) are required to hold a CAP (vocational certificate) in catering, which is not the case for foreign cuisines. Strange, isn't it? Intentional or overlooked? I leave the question to you.

Generally speaking—and without going into detail, as such an effort would be unimaginable—we must return to the grand principles of law, to common sense, and sweep away all norms and rules that do nothing but enable the micromanagement by authorities and hinder positive personal initiative, all while creating a dreadful entrepreneurial climate for anyone who wants to take pleasure in building their activity and inefficient in addressing crime and preserving peace.

The High Judiciary Council

The number of breaches committed by this council against the freedom of information is staggering. It is from here that all political assassinations of serious opponents are ordered, since you will be immediately placed under phone surveillance, and they will surely find something to sway public opinion. One might think of the express judicial procedure that François Fillon was subjected to—so starkly contrasting with the usual slowness of all other initiated proceedings—which raises questions. And of course, one might think of the Outreau affair, which is perhaps the most obvious and symptomatic case of a justice system under the control of an invisible mafia of child traffickers: the appointment and administrative harassment of a young and courageous investigative judge for this complex case; the media coverage that put the victims in the dock; the defense orchestrated by Dupont-Moretti, who was later rewarded with the post of Minister of Justice—everything will come to light, don't worry.

The "Wall of Idiots" (Mur des cons) proved that the High Council of the Judiciary is anything but impartial, totally submissive to political representatives and financial powers. It must be dismantled as soon as possible, as it is, in the end, the guarantor of the prevailing chaos.

Punishment and the Death Penalty

I said in the previous volume that there would come a time to judge the judges, and a time to judge the media. In order to build a society, it is necessary to instill fear in the wicked; it's as old as the world and works quite well, as we've seen on several occasions in the Philippines, or more recently in El Salvador. Reinstating the death penalty for some of the most serious crimes—such as cold-blooded murder and juvenile pimping—seems perfectly appropriate. Implement immediate minimum sentences; authorize the police to use legitimate violence and to show creativity in punishment. Use the army to finally tackle the overly visible presence of mafias. A video is circulating online: it's in Brazil, a man is filmed stealing from an old lady—the police draw their guns and kill him, to the great joy of the bystanders. Unfortunately, the people only understand blood; if it is not the blood of the guilty that we shed, it will be that of the innocent. Let us rather shed the blood of the guilty, as it balances the karmic function and satisfies man's primitive instinct.

The Funding of NGOs

NGOs funded by public money must demonstrate perfect transparency, as they are private organizations benefiting from state largesse.

All of their data, the use of resources, physical premises, and their projects must be easily accessible to all citizens. The names of employees, just as in the public service, must be displayed via a mandatory photo badge allowing the identification of the worker during working hours. Participation in the form of volunteering must be made punctual with the same identification, and simple enough to allow immediate control over the activity of these organizations, which will also benefit from the labor of people on welfare (RSA) who choose to do their daily hours there—even on closure days.

Public service premises and sites must be equipped with surveillance systems as a priority, ahead of the monitoring of living spaces, streets, and businesses, while respecting privacy rules. Thus, a restaurant is a private-public living space, while an association funded by the public is a public living space and must be equipped first with surveillance systems.

Military Service and a new Elite of Consciousness

As we have seen, we are facing a spiritual crisis coupled with a crisis of living together. The mandatory military/civic service lasting two years, after the abolition of the parasitic and warmongering bureaucracy, will offer a valuable solution to the lack of shared experience and serve as an initiatory rite of passage where each young person can discover soul, through practical experience. Obviously, in the context of a war with Russia, this project seems rather unappealing, since no one wants to go to the meat grinder or have their organs stolen to enrich Zelensky or Macron—and least of all the soldiers. Military service has always been something that brings people together: it is an individual sacrifice for the collective good.

One must not think of this service as preparation for death, but as preparation for life. Military service will make it possible to develop the great dream of a European army, an army that is above all defensive and humanitarian, which will allow the learning of languages, cultures, and European civilizations through detachments and international exercises. These exercises may range from building a bridge, to restoring an old building, to humanitarian missions with disaster-stricken populations.

Such missions will constitute shared histories with long-term positive outcomes and a sustained, even profitable, operation thanks to training in trades that European nations will need. It will be possible to substitute military service with a Civic service to train the required administration, or even a spiritual service to train the new class of sages and healers, in order to establish the future elite of consciousness.

Old Cities vs. Modern Cities

The often-mentioned opposition between old cities and modern cities only makes sense if one refuses to see the opportunity that lies in thinking of urban planning as a living continuation rather than a functional rupture. While modern cities have often been designed with an obsession for efficiency, strict zoning, and the separation of functions (living, producing, circulating), old cities bear witness to an organic intelligence, where each construction fits into an evolving, adaptable, human fabric.

In the face of the housing crisis, the abandonment of certain city centers, and the growing inefficiency of bureaucratic urbanism, it is necessary to initiate a pragmatic and circular refoundation of our urban territories. This refoundation involves abandoning rigid quotas of social housing, often imposed blindly, and reinvesting unused public buildings, particularly in historic centers. These places, rich in history and collective anchoring, must become homes of life once more.

The intelligent transformation of these existing structures can be achieved through public-private initiatives, but also through the mobilization of military and civic services, which will participate in the rehabilitation of provincial heritage, disused industrial sites, or obsolete administrative buildings. These actions will have the dual effect of recreating urban diversity while training younger generations in the realities of work, territory, and transmission.

As a transitional measure, temporary housing could be allocated to homeless individuals who wish to engage in a reintegration pathway, by actively participating in these reconstruction projects, under the supervision of an operational project leader. This model reconciles social requirements, economic efficiency, and the valorization of heritage. It restores a dignity of actors to those too often reduced to dependency.

Thus, starting from the ancient heart of cities and moving toward their peripheries, according to a circular and regenerative logic, it becomes possible to invent a city of the future that is no longer a technocratic monster, but a living organism, nourished by memory, solidarity, and collective intelligence.

Operative Freemasonry

While speculative Freemasonry, detached from reality, increasingly seems to weigh on the fluidity of the State and the social utility of institutions, it becomes necessary to imagine an operative alternative, rooted in practice and initiation through action. This new model, inspired by the ancient guilds of trades, could find its place within a renewed civic and military structure, where learning, service, and transmission would be the pillars of authentic elevation, both individual and collective.

This operative Freemasonry, thus conceived, would be distinguished by its concrete dimension: it would be organized into professional corps linked to major national and European projects — restoration of heritage, sustainable technologies, social engineering, infrastructure. Each member would progress through a natural hierarchy, based on skill, experience, and contribution to common works. Initiation would no longer be symbolic, but productive and lived, giving meaning to fraternity through the shared task.

The speculative part would not disappear, but would be reimagined: it would take the form of courses of consciousness, where members would study, among other things, Jung's *Red Book*, Ancient Greek, and the spiritual tradition of their choice, in a spirit of fruitful confrontation of wisdoms. Far from a flat syncretism, this interior plurality would allow for a mutual enrichment of religions, philosophies, and worldviews. Moral consciousness would thus be the foundation of practical competence, not its ornament.

Within this framework, the pursuit of immediate financial profitability would be deliberately kept at a distance. The projects undertaken would be evaluated according to their qualitative radiance, sustainable efficiency, social impact, structural innovations, and the systemic economies they enable. The aim would not be to produce fast and in bulk, but to produce rightly and well: architecture of meaning, engineering of civilization.

Such a structure would also allow for a fluid and coherent transmission of major collective projects, from the popular will (referendums), through Parliament, to their monarchical guarantee. In an age of artificial intelligence, where design and communication are automated, this operative Freemasonry would be capable of reducing bureaucratic downtime, mobilizing skills immediately, and launching fully controlled projects from end to end.

Thus, would be born a new elite: no longer a closed or speculative caste, but an aristocracy of action, meaning, and service.

Borders, Integration, and "Social Nationalism"

At the risk of being labelled a Nazi or Basque separatist, I highlight the *Lauburu*, the Basque cross, which is a swastika with rounded edges, or a rounded-angled hooked cross. It is undeniable that Hitler had some economic success in implementing German National Socialism, but he made the grave error of attributing to it a racial aspect which today, in our diverse societies, has no place.

Indeed, I believe we are fully ready to build a society with the people present; no matter where they come from; but the prerequisite would be to regain control of our borders, because it is impossible to build society when an incessant flow of newcomers, whom we do not have time to properly integrate into our existing societies, generates insecurity and causes the flight of our former French, who would be the most able to transmit the spirit and culture; whether they be Normans, Basques, Vietnamese, or Moroccans.

France has always been a country of differentiated assimilation, both at home and abroad: neither imposed monoculture nor fragmented multiculturalism, but a balance to be found between sharing customs, intergenerational transmission, and respect for external contributions.

Return of Craftsmanship and Local Cultures

It is striking to see the originality and diversity of local cultures, even just in Aquitaine. Our ancestors fully understood the need for differentiation, and they expressed it in their clothing, their customs, and the practice of their trades. It is very regrettable that globalization and industry have led to the disappearance of most of the textile manufacturing, because it is in textiles and the pride of dress that this differentiation is most clearly expressed. When you travel in Central America or Asia, you frequently encounter grandmothers who continue to practice their craft religiously—whether weaving, sewing, or transforming local material into a usable substance. There, the elder remains useful, transmitting know-how, tradition, and continuing to produce. They have their place, and the community takes care to feed them and entertain them.

We note a certain return to traditional, local, and differentiated textiles with brands like Katxi Clothing, which reclaim symbols of Basque identity while adapting textiles to modern fashions. But is it going far enough? A spiritual revolution should be accompanied by the material, and weddings as well as funerals should be identifiable, with garments ordered well in advance, unique handmade pieces from noble and rare materials, examples of which can be observed at the Château de Lourdes.

Why not consider the development of regional tartans, since there was a time when the kilt was worn in the Basque and Béarnaise mountains, and it is a very suitable garment for mountain walking?

After all, production has a social virtue; if we must pay people to do nothing, we might as well develop traditional activities, even if they seem unprofitable at first glance. Unfortunately, it seems that the government as well as the Church are reluctant toward any productive and commercial activity, preferring to appropriate buildings to turn them into museums or offices that bring little in terms of community dynamics, since they are always closed. By stopping production, people slack off, drink, and smoke. If we are to do something, we might as well produce.

The Potlatch and the Village Fair

The potlatch was, among certain Indigenous nations of North America, a fundamental rite: a gift-giving festival where each tribe rivaled in generosity, sacrificing its own productions not to accumulate, but to elevate itself in prestige, moral authority, and influence. This idea struck me during my visit to Lourdes, at the international military festival. There mingled celebration, culture, and religion.

We propose to reactivate this archaic and sacred principle on a European scale. Once a year, as part of the universal military service, a great inter-state ceremony will gather the outgoing regiments from each European country. This will be the European Potlatch: a moment of gift, transmission, and mutual revelation.

Each nation will send its youth, bearers of the gifts of their producers: food, works of art, know-how, performances, technologies, music, machines, traditional clothing, modified vehicles, piloting demonstrations, concerts, mission stories, exhibitions of accomplished achievements. It will be neither a market nor an exhibition, but a sacred competition of gift-giving—where each people will show what they are ready to offer to their youth and neighbors, beyond profit, in the name of honor, beauty, and memory. Hierarchy will not be imposed but will naturally emerge from

generosity, creativity, and the greatness of soul of the participating nations.
This potlatch will have several virtuous effects:
• To create a shared memory among young Europeans through strong, common, festive, and initiatory experiences.
• To elevate the idea of prestige through the demonstration of gift and excellence (artistic, technical, spiritual).
• To revive local cultures by inspiring village festivals, music, and traditions through exchange.
• To put back at the center the productive role of regions, which will each contribute to the gifts offered to the youth.
This rite will become a landmark in the life of every citizen, mixing the feeling of belonging, admiration, and discovery, and founding a Europe of peoples, gestures, and works, far from dry treaties and technocratic injunctions.

Solving the Monetary Problem

The United States has understood this well: they are not going to save the Fed. The money printing press has overheated, and they have taken the reins of the paradigm shift, from which we are taking the exact opposite course. Our elites, attached to an ancestral French model, moreover with this endless war in Ukraine, are leading us toward hyperinflation and the devaluation of savings. The Bretton Woods system is over, the US dollar is no longer the reserve currency, and this absurd floating system is caput mortem. It is not the invention of a European cryptocurrency that will save the sinking ship. The central entity especially does not want to lose control over money creation, but through its international betrayals it has already annihilated the key element of its payment systems and its currency — that is to say, trust. How can one trust the EU after the freezing of Russian assets?
It is necessary to return to a simple and efficient reserve currency system, because debt is simply value-destructive — it is easy to understand.

Bitcoin is rapidly becoming one of the most valued assets in the world. For good reason, it does everything better than centralized payment organizations: faster, cheaper, private. Yet EU countries aligned with Macron, such as Germany or England — although no longer part of it — have in recent years sold all their bitcoin reserves in an absurd loss operation of more than 6 billion, instead of focusing on developing a good European electronic wallet. Consequently, our entire monetary system is running to its doom, and tech giants will win, as has already been the case with Uber, Facebook, YouTube, Airbnb, etc. In the end, we will be left to choose between WeChat and Twitter — in other words, between the US and China... Indeed, Twitter (X) aims to be the future payment system with the possibility of storing digital identities, digital currencies, credit cards, etc. All that is needed is for France and England to take the step and decide to accumulate reserves in bitcoin and gold, through savings, if necessary, but they must do it now. A piece of advice: do it yourselves...

By the way, does anyone know where our gold reserves have gone? I believe Macron has sold everything, and your skin is next.

Solving the Accounting Problem

We suffer in France from an obvious budget imbalance. Therefore, first and foremost, the accounting problem must be addressed. We have a system that promotes exclusion through excessive welfare, and simultaneously an overabundance of a non-uniform public service. It is necessary to rationalize and level the public service to put everyone on the same footing, which includes pensions that weigh far too heavily on the nation's overall structure and on the maintenance of our civilization.

Certain provisions now require RSA (French minimum income benefit) recipients to offer 15 hours of work per week to the government or in the associative sector. This sensible provision brings the French system closer to the Australian social system, much stricter and rigid but well-regulated, offering a simple safety net to the inactive, provided they prove they are seeking employment, accept any job offers made to them, and participate as volunteers in community life. This resolves part of the problem: reintegrating and re-engaging the excluded, making them productive while allowing the growth of public utility associations. The second part of the problem is the huge pool of civil servants, some 5 million. To ensure fair contribution, the RSA should be revalued to the minimum wage of €11.88 per hour, i.e., €712.8 monthly. All roles in public service, at all levels—including ministers and parliamentarians—should see their salaries adjusted to the minimum wage of €11.88 per hour, with a proposed contract exchange of 2 days per week. This remuneration would be complemented by a sum of €200 per month per child under 16 years, per household, starting from the first child. The contract exchange will enable the training of new workers to ensure a sufficient pool of trained personnel to cover all needs. As much as possible, management roles should be eliminated, including office managers, human resources, with recruitment done through a training period and team co-optation. Customer satisfaction will judge the quality of services provided; we will seek "task enrichment" rather than impoverishment and recourse to outside agencies or subcontracting, and personal initiative will be encouraged. The reduction of public contribution to two days a week will increase worker satisfaction by preventing weariness from repetitive tasks, which will be reflected in client satisfaction.

Retirees will be allocated the same sum (€712.88 + housing expenses) and may, if they wish, offer 2 days of volunteering or work to supplement their pension up to its maximum value, as far as their health allows. Preferably, retirees will be assigned teaching roles according to their capacities and desires, favouring generational transfer and social aspects. Rents in senior residences must be capped because there is a resource that is overexploited by unions and building managers, where it is not uncommon to see rents twice as high as standard residences. The difference between the pension of €712.88 (daily expenses) plus rent will be used to ensure the transition to a new pay-as-you-go pension system with a sovereign fund allocated to Bitcoin and Gold. This sovereign fund will guarantee the value reserve of national wealth creation, partly through national production and partly through encouraged individual savings. This model has proven itself in El Salvador and is now promoted by the United States. Once the transition and the new system are stabilized, we can gradually return to "available savings," progressively and in phases, in an equitable sharing so that no one is left penniless to live, although efforts will be necessary from all retirees to restart the new system, which will considerably lighten the burden on the young, the active, and entrepreneurs. A minimum regulatory savings (8% of gross salary in Australia) will be imposed, as well as optional savings.

The key element here is the creation of a contributory national basic income (€712.88), associated with a voluntary contribution obligation under penalty of payment freezing, and voluntary progressive reduction of public contracts to two days per week, with valorization of personal initiative. The entire basic public service is thus leveled (€11.88/h + X per year of seniority), social minimums are maintained, the community is encouraged to do more and the inactive to work.

Free transport and public services for all persons providing their 2 days of weekly work will greatly reduce the need for controllers in public transport. The generalization of the 2-day public contract will allow employees to free time for personal initiatives by facilitating and deregulating the creation of individual businesses, by removing labor regulations, allowing companies to hire much more easily, while greatly reducing the risks they face when hiring a new employee. Immediate cessation of minimum social benefits payments for misconduct or failure to contribute will be the rule. In the near future, "good conduct" will be established in a decentralized manner by a system of smart contracts, customer ratings, or circular evaluation.

Income tax on revenues below €30K will be exempted, as well as capital gains taxes on gold and bitcoin to attract and retain investors in the territory.

One Solution: Operative Monarchy

This system implies the abolition of the republican system, and that is where the problem lies in France. The monarch is neither a tyrant nor a blood heir, but a bearer of the collective destiny, and he bases his legitimacy on a monarchic and consensual pact, not on divine right. Preferably, the monarch is here "called" by the people, or by spiritual authorities, which unfortunately do not exist in France, except for speculative Freemasonry which guarantees... the republic. Do you see the ouroboros?

Here, the monarch swears an oath before the people, the army, tradition, and the future, in a rite of national refoundation, and power is redirected from technocratic consensus toward excellence, commitment, and transcendence. The nation is no longer subject to abstract laws but to an embodied leadership, governed by operativity, justice, and merit.

Preferably, on a symbolic level, the monarch should sit doubly at Saint Germain-en-Laye, to separate himself from the Macron/Sun King symbolism, and at Pau to mark the decentralization of the state and in memory of the good King Henry IV.

It will be necessary to abolish political parties and the worn-out parliamentary representative democracy controlled by the media, which will bring huge savings to the nation. We already paid our famous Tony Estanguet €400,000 for well-run Olympics—why not keep him to establish a long-term plan for sports, or at least as Minister of Sports?

To do this, we will first have to remove Brigitte and Macron with the help of the army, then establish a transitional government maintaining the Prime Minister to ensure stability during the transition, with the consensual appointment of a general, Chief of the Armed Forces, who will be authorized, with the monarch's agreement, to take command of the National Police. During this phase, which lasts four years, we will institute mandatory military service, make illegal unions, semi-public agencies, professional orders, and categorical privileges, and reduce the public service to its strict executive and sovereign role. We will break away from Brussels' authority in law-making while keeping the Euro and reinstating strict border controls for non-Schengen area nationals.

All salaries and pensions of the public service will be capped at €3,000 net per month with no possibility of cumulation to allow competent people, disinterested in finance due to previous careers or a passion for public service, to enter, outside members of the government, senior civil servants, and high-ranking military officers. By relying on the immediate reinstatement of military service and taking control of unused public places, we will quickly achieve stable functioning and train new recruits for the immediate needs of this new renaissance.

Spiritual studies will become immediately mandatory from middle school, and school programs will be strongly reoriented towards craftsmanship, local and national culture, family, and good manners, with decentralization of public-school administrations based on elders, living knowledge, effort, and challenge. Young men and women love traditions and well-placed authority. Mandatory courses from the first year of middle school: philosophy, ancient Greek, introduction to comparative religions, customs, consciousness, and choice of a musical instrument. From age 12, youths will be encouraged to join productive workshops led by military recruits and retirees to foster vocations.

Conclusion: Too Many Public Services Kill the Public Service

Henry IV said: "A people is a beast that lets itself be led by the nose, mainly the Parisians."

As you understand, periodically, the serpent bites its own tail — that is how the Leviathan, the beast, works. The age of Pisces is over; an opportunity for humanity arises through technology, but everything will depend on what we make of it individually above all. The old system, the age of Pisces, is crumbling, and we can imagine a better future — or let it die.But above all, never forget:

"Good cooking and good wine are paradise on Earth," to which I would also add good music and fine clothes.

General Conclusion

If you have followed me this far, you have probably noticed that all things are connected, and that offering a practical answer to hundreds of years of misguidance requires a complete overhaul of our beliefs and the systems that are, whether overtly or covertly, tightly intertwined and manipulated.

Since my soul demanded it, I wished here to sound the alarm and attempt to bring a chipped stone to the edifice, or at least a viable proposal — to restore an ancient oral tradition of studying reality, of symbolism through the texts of our tradition. Along the way, you may have been amused, instructed, or outraged, which is also good, because all this should have made you think and perhaps made you more aware of the unconscious patterns that govern us without our knowledge, patterns that a few groups know by heart. I hope you will no longer remain indifferent to them.

The suspicions I had about Australia led me to England; and there lies a powerful, well-established system that we must acknowledge, if not confront directly — let us be like squirrels; let us shoot arrows; continue the fight; and preserve the tradition.

Contradiction is what defines the world, and the only answer is the union of opposites. That is what God wants from you and me: a feathered snake.

Monas tri una apud Aegyptios.

Omnia ad maiorem Dei Gloriam
Virginisque Matris.

Author, Héraclès Harixcalde

French Australian analyst in strategic intelligence, big data and artificial intelligence applied to mental health services, CEO of *CommUnicorn*, the author advocates for the recognition of electromagnetic harassment and seeks to support its victims. Since the COVID-19 crisis, he has been denouncing the growing disconnect between the results officially reported by institutions and the reality on the ground.

In his view, the root of the problem lies in the design and control of information and organizational systems — structures dominated by key actors under the influence of occult and mafioso powers, within a global extortion network.

This is the third and last volume of the trilogy Mysterium Australis.

BY THE SAME AUTHOR and EDITOR

ALREADY AVAILABLE on BOD

Mysterium Australis I – Kubrick and the Deep State
Mysterium Australis II – Logan's Apocalypse: How to catch a Leviathan?

FUTURE RELEASES

Héraclès Harixcalde – The Tale of the Squirrel King
Eliza Logan – Restalrig Series
Eliza Logan – Saint Johnstoun, John, Earl of Gowrie Series